DINNERS FOR TWO

SHARON O'CONNOR'S

DINNERS FOR TWO

Menus and Music
Volume IV

Recipes from
Romantic Country Inns

Music by the
San Francisco String Quartet

Drawings by John Coreris

Menus and Music Productions, Inc.
Piedmont, California

The Fearrington House recipes on pages 39-46 are from *The Fearrington House Cookbook* by

   Jenny Fitch, published by Ventana Press, Chapel Hill, North Carolina.

The Milllcroft Inn recipes on pages 159-165 are from *The Millcroft Inn Cookbook* by

   Fredy Stamm, published by Porcupine's Quill, Erin, Ontario.

Library of Congress Cataloging-in-Publication Data

O'Connor, Sharon

Menus and Music™

Dinners for Two

Recipes from Romantic Country Inns

Music by the San Francisco String Quartet

Drawings by John Coreris

Includes Index

1. Cookery 2. Entertaining 3. Menus

I. Title: Dinners for Two

91-090 290

ISBN 0-9615150-5-8 (paperback)

ISBN 1-883914-07-8 (hardcover)

Menus and Music is published by

Menus and Music Productions, Inc.

1462 66th Street

Emeryville, CA 94608

(510) 658-9100

Book and cover design by Jacqueline Jones Design

Cover photograph of The Point on Saranac Lake, New York, by Geoffrey Clifford

Manufactured in the United States of America

10 9 8

CONTENTS

5

ACKNOWLEDGMENTS

I would like to thank the many people who made this volume possible.

To Nathan Rubin, James Shallenberger, and the late David George, fellow members of the San Francisco String Quartet. To Martha Rubin of Fog City Sound, and Ron Davis at Mastertrack Productions, for musical production and support.

My deepest gratitude to all the chefs, proprietors, and managing directors of the inns and resorts who generously contributed menus and recipes to the cookbook. I want especially to thank Maurice Nayrolles at Meadowood Resort Hotel for his support; the Twilight Concerts at Meadowood are a dream come true.

To my editor, Carolyn Miller, once again thanks for being so flexible and attentive to detail. To Lori Merish for more than two years of work sustained by peanut butter sandwiches.

To Jacqueline Jones and Kristen Jester, for their wonderful design and for supporting this project so enthusiastically.

To Jean Harrell, for her steadiness and sweet good humor; to Ned Waring, pianist extraordinaire and wit beyond compare; and the rest of the crew.

To Claire and Caitlin, the joys of my life, and most of all to John Coreris, for his beautiful drawings and his love.

INTRODUCTION

Some of the happiest moments of my life have been spent at dinners for two! Sharing an intimate dinner of fine food is one of the great civilized pleasures, and enhancing it with beautiful music makes the moment even richer.

During one of my not too difficult research assignments (dining on glorious food at an inn surrounded by spectacular countryside), I was enjoying the beautiful recorded classical music during dinner. I realized that this would probably not have been the case ten years ago. Then it was quite common for a good restaurant to play music in the background that sounded like soggy overcooked canned vegetables instead of the fresh crisp-tender vegetables we enjoy today. There has been a wonderful revolution in sensiblities! The quality and choice of background music has improved as well as the quality and freshness of food.

Menus and Music has packaged up my life; I play music professionally and love cooking and fine food. I founded the San Francisco String Quartet in 1975, and we have been performing dinner music in the Sheraton-Palace Hotel's Garden Court for the past twelve years. As people nourish themselves, we've been nurturing a love of chamber music. The musical program recorded here includes some of my favorites from the chamber music repertoire and can be enjoyed during your kitchen preparations, while you are dining, or as an after dinner concert.

The contributors to this book have provided you with a connoisseur's guide to inns in the United States, Canada, and Bermuda. Most of them are members of Relais & Chateaux, a thirty-six-year-old association of 377 highly individual deluxe hotels and gourmet restaurants in thirty-seven countries throughout the world. These privately owned accommodations, most in country surroundings, reflect the personality and dedication of the hotelier as well as the region in which they are located. Relais & Chateaux members have all met very exacting entry requirements and share a steadfast commitment to the five C's of Relais & Chateaux hospitality: Character, Courtesy, Calm, Charm, and Cuisine.

It was inspiring to learn that each inn is a realized dream that began with the owner's personal passion and a desire to be the best. I am honored to have made the acquaintance of twenty amazing chefs from these inns during the past two years. I think you will appreciate their talent, expertise, and creativity.

This volume of *Menus and Music* is a ticket for an excursion to some of the most romantic destinations in North America via the kitchen in your own home. These inns are all quite small, and there is a real warmth and authenticity to them. The chefs are guardians of a regional heritage, and they serve authentic country cooking rendered with imagination and subtlety. Their wonderful regional diversity will allow you to savor a Napa Valley Menu from Meadowood Resort Hotel in the California wine country, a menu of Fruits of the Maine Coastline from the White Barn Inn in Maine, or a Holiday Menu from The Inn at Little Washington in Virginia. All of the chefs scour their environs to find top quality ingredients, which allows them to explore innovative regional cuisines rather than serving the same monotonous specialties. At the same time, home cooks now enjoy an availability of foods unknown to most of us ten or fifteen years ago and this makes such ethnic, exotic, and regional dishes accessible to us all.

You can recreate an entire menu from this book or choose dishes from several inns to create your own sampler. Composing a menu and cooking it are somewhat like orchestrating a piece of music: lots of different elements have to work together collectively. A meal engages all the senses. Taste, of course, is primary, but aroma, color, texture, and sound also should be part of the enjoyment. You can mix and match the recipes with your own favorites or create your own menu as long as you achieve an equilibrium.

Introduction

You may increase the amounts in the recipes if you are planning a dinner party for four or six. I have tested many of these recipes at dinner parties for eight. I suggest that you make as much ahead as possible and keep everything waiting in your refrigerator until just before your dinner. Remember to freeze stocks, and double other recipes, if you wish, to keep for other occasions.

This book includes indulgences that require rationing; they are for special occasions, and when that occasion comes, enjoy every mouthful! I think it's better to have a small helping of something really tremendous than a lot of something that isn't nearly as tasty.

The menus and recipes in this volume are for those occasions when you want to enjoy the leisurely preparation of a romantic dinner. Today both men and women are likely to be competent in the kitchen and to enjoy cooking. You can have fun making these recipes together, secluding yourself at home, and savoring a relaxing interlude.

So here's to fine food and beautiful music together! I hope this volume of *Menus and Music* will help you create the right ambience for a wonderfully romantic dinner. Creating this moment will be well worth it; it's one of the things that makes life worth living. The chef, whether in a restaurant or the home, is a maker of fantasies; so enjoy making your own!

–Sharon O'Connor

NOTES ABOUT THE COMPOSERS

Johann Sebastian Bach (1685–1750)
Air from Orchestral Suite in D Major, BWV 1068
"Jesu, Joy of Man's Desiring"

Johann Sebastian Bach combined outstanding performing musicianship with supreme creative powers, inventiveness, and intellectual control. As a virtuoso, he achieved legendary fame in his lifetime, and as a composer he holds a unique historical position. He mastered and surpassed the techniques, styles, and general musical achievements of his own and earlier generations, and his works have been used by later ages in a great variety of ways. The transcribed movement recorded here from the Orchestral Suite was composed in about 1720. The Air is one of the best known of Bach's compositions. It was popularized by the nineteenth-century violinist August Wilhemj, who transposed it down a ninth and transcribed it for violin and piano as "Air on the G String." "Jesu, Joy of Man's Desiring" is a chorale tune from Bach's Cantata 147.

Alfredo Catalini (1854–1893)
"Ebben, n'andro lontano" from *La Wally*

Catalani was an opera composer whose compositions were at the edge of mainstream Italian opera during the last quarter of the nineteenth century. He had an instinct for high Romanticism and a penchant for libretti involving duels. The piece transcribed here for string quartet is the best known aria from his opera *La Wally*, which premiered at La Scala in 1892. The great conductor Toscanini named his daughter after the heroine of this work. This aria was used as the musical score for the movie *Diva*.

Frederic Chopin (1810–1849)
Nocturne, Op. 9, No. 2

    Chopin was a Polish composer who combined an extraordinary gift for melody, an adventurous harmonic sense, an intuitive understanding of formal design, and a brilliant piano technique in composing a large body of piano music. One of the leading nineteenth-century composers, his music represents the quintessence of the Romantic piano tradition, and his music embodies more fully than that of any other composer the expressive and technical characteristics of this instrument. A Chopin nocturne isolates a right-hand melody, allowing the fullest possible expression in its playing, while the left hand provides the entire rhythmic and harmonic background in broken chord accompaniment. The Nocturne transcribed here for string quartet gives the melody exclusively to the first violin and the chordal accompaniment to the second violin, viola, and cello.

Notes About the Composers

Jeremiah Clarke (1674–1707)
"Prince of Denmark's March"

      Clarke was an English composer and organist who is mainly remembered as a composer for the church, but he also wrote songs, incidental music for the theater, and harpsichord pieces. "The Prince of Denmark's March" is his best known work, although it has been mistakenly known as "Trumpet Voluntary" by Purcell. Sir Henry Wood made a celebrated arrangement of Clarke's piece for trumpet, organ, and drums, entitled it "Trumpet Voluntary," and ascribed it to Purcell. Wood probably made his arrangement from a nineteenth-century organ arrangement that attributed the original to Purcell, because the composition had appeared as a harpsichord piece in a group of anonymous items preceded and followed by pieces by Purcell. Clarke contributed his "Prince of Denmark's March" to *A Choice Collection of Ayres for the Harpsichord* (1700), and it also appears in a suite of pieces for wind instruments by Clarke.

The Prince of Denmark's March: Round O

George Frederick Handel (1685–1759)
Finale from *Water Music*

Handel, a naturalized English composer of German birth, was one of the greatest composers of the Baroque age. His *Water Music* was probably first performed on July 17, 1717. King George I and his courtiers, followed by a large number of boats, sailed on the Thames from Whitehall to Chelsea, where they had supper, then returned by the same route at three in the morning. At the king's request, a second barge containing fifty musicians played works specially composed for the occasion by Handel. The music was a great success, according to an account sent to Prussia two days later: "His Majesty approved of it so greatly that he caused it to be repeated three times in all, although each performance lasted an hour—namely twice before and once after supper."

Josif Ivanovici (1845–1902)
"Anniversary Waltz"

Ivanovici was a Romanian composer and conductor who wrote fanfares, marches, waltzes, and potpourris of folk melodies that were popular at the soirées of his day. His "Danube Waves," which is also called "Anniversary Waltz," has become widely known.

Wolfgang Amadeus Mozart (1756–1791)
Divertimento I, K.136
"Romanza" from *Eine Kleine Nachtmusik*

Mozart is regarded as the most universal composer in the history of Western music. He excelled in every musical medium current in his time, especially chamber music for strings, the piano concerto, and opera. Mozart composed three Divertimenti in 1772. The term *divertimento* implies performance by a small ensemble, one to a part, and the three movements of the Divertmento I

recorded here are solo rather than orchestral music. *Eine Kleine Nachtmusik*
(*A Little Night Music*) was composed in 1787 while Mozart was in the midst of
writing the opera *Don Giovanni*, but no details survive as to why it was written.
This serenade is one of Mozart's most perfectly crafted miniatures and is also
probably the most widely played piece of those he composed for strings. It was
written for string quartet and bass, but can be successfully performed by a string
quartet, since the bass and cello share the bass line.

Johann Pachelbel (1653–1706)
Canon in D

Pachelbel was a German organist and composer of organ and harpsichord
music as well as a leading composer of Protestant church music. His fondness for
the variation form is demonstrated by his composition of six canons. The San
Francisco String Quartet's version of his Canon in D, based on eight notes played
by the cello that remain unaltered throughout, starts with a single violin line
repeated identically (after a two-bar wait) by the second violin and, after another
two-bar wait, by the viola.

Notes About the Composers

Antonio Vivaldi (1687–1741)
First Movement of "Spring," from *The Four Seasons*

Vivaldi was the first great violin virtuoso, and the father of the modern concerto. He made the instrument a star performer by his own innovative virtuosity and by modifying the concerto grosso form to allow the violin (and other instruments as well) to function as a solo voice singing out over the orchestra. Vivaldi wrote as many as five hundred concertos for various kinds of instruments. He was also a pioneer of orchestral programme music such as his four concertos portraying the seasons, which he composed in 1725. Printed with *The Four Seasons* was a quartet of sonnets, one for each concerto. The poet is unknown, but could easily have been Vivaldi himself, who may have intended the sonnets as a guide to the pictorial content of the music. The first two stanzas of the following poem describe the movement recorded here by the San Francisco String Quartet.

Spring

Spring has come and joyfully
the birds greet her with merry song,
and brooks blown by the breezes,
sweetly murmuring, begin to flow.

Then come, covering the air with a black mantle,
lightning and thunder, chosen to herald her,
and when they cease, the tiny birds
take up again their enchanting song.

And after, on the pleasant, flowery meadow,
to the cherished sough of leafy boughs,
sleeps the goatherd with his faithful
dog at his side.

To the joyous sound of the pastoral pipe,
nymphs and shepherds dance in the
beloved cottage
at the shining appearance of spring.

Notes About the Composers

AUBERGE DU SOLEIL

Rutherford, California

Auberge du Soleil is an extraordinary restaurant and inn set on thirty-three acres of hillside overlooking the Napa Valley in the California wine country. The Auberge began as the vision of San Francisco restaurateur Claude Rouas. He and his design team first created the fine restaurant, which includes a wraparound terrace allowing guests to lunch in dappled sunlight or dine by the light of the moon. The hillside orchard of olive and oak trees was then terraced to accommodate Mediterranean-style maisons, each housing a number of very comfortable suites with spectacular views of the vineyards below and the Mayacamas Mountains beyond. Tennis courts, a spa, and an Olympic-size swimming pool complete this superb retreat. Guests at the inn can enjoy golf, horseback riding, cycling, and tours and tasting sessions at the world-famous vineyards and wineries close by. Besides membership in Relais & Chateaux, Auberge du Soleil has received a Four-Star Award from the Mobil Travel Guide.

Auberge du Soleil's romantic restaurant joins classic French cuisine with Californian innovations. The menu is as imaginative as the contemporary paintings and graceful architecture of the dining room. Chef Udo Nechutnys created the following dinner for two for *Menus and Music*.

THE MENU

Auberge du Soleil

Crab Cakes with Green Pea Sauce

Spicy Squash Soup

Steamed Fish with Napa Cabbage,
Shiitake Mushrooms, and Chinese Black Beans

Pepe's Citrus Meringue Tart

Crab Cakes with Green Pea Sauce

¼ red bell pepper, cored and seeded
1 teaspoon unsalted butter
3 ounces fresh cooked Dungeness crab meat
½ shallot, chopped
2 tablespoons Dry Sack sherry
Salt and pepper to taste
2 ounces fillet of sole
1 large egg yolk
2 tablespoons heavy (whipping) cream
2 large egg whites
Green Pea Sauce (recipe follows)
½ small tomato, peeled, seeded, cut into julienne,
and lightly seasoned with salt and pepper

Peel the bell pepper by laying it flat and removing the skin with a vegetable peeler. Mince and set aside.

In a sauté pan or skillet, melt the butter over medium heat and sauté the shallot for 1 minute. Stir in the bell pepper and continue cooking for 1 minute. Add the sherry and cook over medium-high heat until the liquid has nearly evaporated. Remove from the heat and cool; then place in a mixing bowl and blend in the crab, salt, and pepper, and set aside.

In a blender or food processor, blend the fillet of sole and egg yolk; then gradually add the heavy cream and continue blending. Do not overmix, or the cream will turn to butter. Season with salt and pepper, and stir into the crab mixture. In a large bowl, whip the egg whites until they form stiff peaks, then fold into the crab mixture. Cover and chill in the refrigerator for at least 30 minutes.

Auberge du Soleil

Preheat the oven to 375° F. Line a baking sheet with parchment paper and lightly butter it, or butter the baking sheet generously. Butter two 3-inch pastry or poaching rings* (½ inch high) and set them on the baking sheet. Fill each ring with the crab mixture and bake for 10 minutes. Run a sharp knife around each baking ring and unmold the crab cakes upside down.

Serving. Pour a pool of green pea sauce on each of 2 salad plates. Place a crab cake, with browned side up, on each pool of sauce and garnish with the julienne of tomato.

*In place of poaching rings, you can use clean tuna cans with both ends removed.

Green Pea Sauce
½ cup shelled fresh or thawed frozen peas
3 fresh mint leaves
1 tablespoon heavy (whipping) cream
Salt and pepper to taste
Pinch of sugar
¼ cup dry white wine or clam juice

In a small saucepan, blanch the peas for 1 minute in boiling salted water. Remove the peas with a slotted spoon and plunge them into cold water to set the color; drain.

In a blender or food processor, place the blanched peas and mint and purée. Transfer to a small saucepan, add the clam juice or wine and cream, and cook gently over low heat. Season with salt, pepper, and sugar.

Auberge du Soleil

Spicy Squash Soup

1 winter squash (such as butternut)
1 tablespoon butter
2 small yellow onions, diced
1 mild chili pepper, cored, seeded, and cut into small dice
1 quart Chicken Stock (page 220) or canned chicken broth
1 tablespoon whole cumin seed
Salt and pepper to taste
Unsweetened whipped cream for garnish
½ cup toasted pine nuts for garnish

Preheat the oven to 375° F. Cut the squash in half and scrape out all the pulp and seeds. Place the squash face down in a baking pan with enough water to cover the bottom of the pan, and bake in the preheated oven until soft, about 45 minutes. Peel off and discard the skin, reserve the pan and juices, and set the squash aside.

In a large saucepan or a stock pot, melt the butter and sauté the onions and chili pepper over low heat. Add the cooked squash and pan juices to the onions; then add the chicken stock or broth and bring to a simmer.

Meanwhile, in a hot, dry saucepan, toast the cumin seeds over medium-high heat until golden brown. Toast the pine nuts in the same fashion and set them aside. Using a mortar and pestle, grind the toasted cumin seeds to a fine powder, then add to the soup. Season the soup with salt and pepper.

Serving. Pour the hot soup into 2 shallow soup bowls. Garnish with a dollop of lightly whipped cream and some toasted pine nuts.

Auberge du Soleil

Steamed Fish with Napa Cabbage, Shiitake Mushrooms, and Chinese Black Beans

½ head Napa cabbage, cored and chopped
Two 6-ounce flatfish fillets (such as fluke or halibut)
4 ounces shiitake mushrooms, cut into quarters
¼ cup olive oil
2 tablespoons chopped shallots
2 garlic cloves, minced
2 tablespoons finely grated fresh ginger
1 ounce Chinese salted black beans, rinsed
Minced green onions for garnish
Cilantro sprigs for garnish

Preheat the oven to 400° F. Spread a sheet of parchment paper on a flat working surface and brush the edges with oil. On one half of the sheet, place a portion of the cabbage in the center, place a fillet on top of the cabbage, and arrange the mushrooms around; fold the remaining half of the parchment over the fish, and secure by folding in the edges. Repeat with the other sheet of parchment. Place the parchment packages on a baking sheet and bake just until the fish is cooked, 8 to 10 minutes. Remove from the oven and transfer to a plate.

In a sauté pan or skillet, heat the olive oil and sauté the shallots, garlic, ginger, and black beans for about 3 minutes.

Serving. Remove the fish from their parchment, transfer to dinner plates, and drizzle the sautéed mixture over. Garnish with green onions and cilantro.

Pepe's Citrus Meringue Tart

1 recipe Pie Pastry (page 225)
2 teaspoons grated lemon zest (page 86)
2 oranges
1 lemon
½ cup sugar
Dash vanilla extract
4 large eggs, separated
1 teaspoon powdered sugar

Preheat the oven to 350° F. Prepare the pastry dough, mixing the zest into the flour. Roll out and use to line an 8-inch tart pan. Crimp the edges. Bake the pastry shell for 20 minutes; unmold and let cool on a rack.

Score the skin of 1 of the oranges and the lemon in quarters and pull off the peel. Place the peel in a saucepan, cover with water, and bring to a boil; drain. Repeat the blanching process twice; this removes any chemicals that may be on the skin and reduces the bitterness. Cut all the white pith and covering membrane from both of the oranges and the lemon. Cupping the fruit in one hand, cut between the membranes and let the fruit sections fall into a bowl. Transfer to a blender or food processor, add the blanched peel, and purée. Add ¼ cup of the sugar, the vanilla, and egg yolks; blend. Transfer to a double boiler and whisk over simmering water for 10 minutes, or until the custard thickens.

Reduce the oven heat to 325° F. Return the tart shell to its pan, pour the custard filling into the shell, and bake for 15 minutes, or until set. Remove from the oven and let cool.

Lower the oven temperature to 300° F. In a large bowl, beat the egg whites until they start to hold their shape; add the remaining ¼ cup of the sugar and continue beating until stiff. Transfer the meringue to a pastry bag fitted with a large star tube. Starting at the center of the tart, pipe meringue in a tight spiral shape over

Auberge du Soleil

the entire surface, placing the circles of meringue close together. Decorate with rosettes around the edge and in the center. Sift powdered sugar over the surface of the tart and bake for 8 minutes, or until the meringue peaks are golden.

Serving. Let the tart cool to room temperature and cut into sixths to serve.

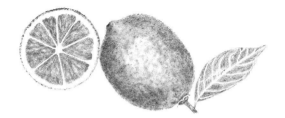

BLANTYRE

Lenox, Massachusetts

Blantyre is a lovingly restored 1902 manor house where visitors feel like houseguests in a more graceful era. The spacious estate is set amid eighty-five acres of woodland and formal lawns in the Berkshire Mountains. Owners Senator and Mrs. John Fitzpatrick have restored Blantyre to its original grandeur. The Tudor-style main house with its leaded-glass windows, sweeping staircase, and immense fireplace includes intimate parlors with heirloom furnishings, a music room that holds a full-sized harp and a Steinway grand piano, and eight handsomely decorated guest rooms. The estate's charming Carriage House provides twelve additional rooms, and several small cottages on the property add four more rooms.

Blantyre's grounds include an outdoor heated swimming pool, a hot tub and sauna, four Har-Tru tennis courts, and two croquet lawns of tournament quality for leisurely or lively recreation. The Berkshires have inspired generations of American writers, artists, and musicians. Tanglewood, the summer home of the Boston Symphony; the Clark Art Institute; summer theaters; and delightful villages with galleries, shops, and restaurants are all nearby.

Blantyre's elegant paneled dining room offers a menu of classically prepared dishes. Blantyre chef Steve Taub created the following dinner for two for *Menus and Music.*

THE MENU

Blantyre

Lamb Ravioli in Rosemary Consommé

*Gâteau of Marinated Salmon with
Cucumber Salad, Crème Fraîche, and Caviar*

*Field Salad with Tart Apple
and Champagne Vinaigrette*

*Fillet of Black Angus Beef with
a Raisin, Pepper, and Armagnac Sauce*

*Praline and Armagnac Mousse with
Caramel Sauce*

Lamb Ravioli in Rosemary Consommé

Rosemary Consommé

5 pounds lamb bones

1 large carrot, peeled

1 celery stalk

1 small onion

*2 each parsley and thyme sprigs, 1 bay leaf, and
4 peppercorns wrapped in cheesecloth and tied*

1 teaspoon tomato purée

Chicken Stock (page 220) or canned chicken broth to cover

Salt and pepper to taste

4 ounces lamb

1 small leek

4 mushrooms

1 small carrot, peeled and chopped

3 egg whites

2 rosemary sprigs

Salt and pepper to taste

Preheat the oven to 400° F. In a baking pan, place the lamb bones and roast them for 15 to 20 minutes, until well browned. Transfer the bones to a stock pot. Coarsely chop the vegetables and add them to the pot along with the herbs, tomato purée, and chicken stock or broth. Season to taste. Bring to a boil, skim the surface with a spoon to remove any foam, and simmer for 2 to 3 hours until the stock is full-flavored, skimming every hour. Strain the stock through a fine sieve.

Coarsely chop the lamb and vegetables in a blender or a food processor, finely chop the lamb and vegetables. Stir in the egg whites. In a large, heavy saucepan, place the lamb and vegetable mixture and the hot stock; bring to a simmer over low heat, stirring constantly. Move the pot so that it sits halfway on the burner and simmer, undisturbed, for 1 hour. Gently ladle the broth through a fine sieve without disturbing the foam on the surface. Place the rosemary in a container and pour the hot consommé over; allow to cool. Season with salt and pepper.

Note: The consommé can be prepared a few days before serving, covered and refrigerated.

Lamb Ravioli

1 teaspoon olive oil
½ teaspoon chopped shallot
2 tablespoons minced red bell pepper
4 ounces ground lean lamb
½ teaspoon chopped fresh rosemary
½ teaspoon chopped fresh parsley
Salt and freshly ground white pepper to taste
12 wonton wrappers
Rosemary sprigs for garnish

In a sauté pan or skillet, heat the olive oil over medium heat and sauté the shallot until translucent. Add the red pepper and sauté an additional 2 minutes. In a mixing bowl, combine the sautéed vegetables, lamb, rosemary, parsley, and salt and pepper. Spread 6 of the wonton wrappers out on a flat work surface. Spoon 1 teaspoon of the filling onto each wonton. Brush the edge of each with water and cover with a second wrapper, pressing the edges tightly together to seal.

In a large saucepan, bring lightly salted water to a boil, and poach the ravioli for 1 to 2 minutes.

Serving. Place 3 ravioli in each of 2 soup bowls and ladle the hot consommé over. Garnish with sprigs of rosemary.

Gâteau of Marinated Salmon with
Cucumber Salad, Crème Fraîche, and Caviar

Marinated Salmon

¼ teaspoon grated lemon zest (page 86)
½ teaspoon chopped fresh dill
½ teaspoon sugar
Salt and freshly ground white pepper to taste
One 4-ounce salmon fillet

In a small mixing bowl, combine the lemon zest, dill, sugar, and salt, and rub this mixture onto the salmon fillet. Wrap the coated salmon fillet in plastic wrap, and refrigerate for at least 8 hours.

Cucumber Salad

½ cucumber, peeled, seeded, and thinly sliced
½ teaspoon salt
½ teaspoon champagne vinegar
1 tablespoon olive oil
Freshly ground pepper to taste

Place the cucumber slices in a colander, sprinkle the salt over, and allow to sit for 30 minutes. Rinse under cold water and pat dry with paper towels. Place the cucumber slices in a small bowl with the vinegar, oil, and ground pepper.

Gâteau Mixture

Marinated Salmon, above
½ teaspoon Crème Fraîche (page 221) or sour cream
Dash of Dijon mustard
2 tablespoons fresh lemon juice

Thirty minutes before serving, rinse the salmon, pat it dry with a towel, and chop it into ⅛-inch cubes. Place the salmon in a small bowl, and stir in the crème fraîche or sour cream, mustard, lemon juice, salt, and pepper. Place in the refrigerator to chill.

Assembling and Serving the Gâteau

Prepared gateau mixture
¼ cup Crème Fraîche (page 221) or sour cream
Prepared cucumber salad
1 lemon
1 tablespoon caviar for garnish
Dill sprigs for garnish

Serving. Chill 2 small salad plates. Place a 3-inch round pastry cutter in the center of 1 plate and fill it with salmon mixture, pressing gently with the back of a spoon. Top with half of the créme fraîche or sour cream and smooth with a spatula. Carefully lift off the pastry cutter. Repeat for the second serving. Surround the salmon with overlapping cucumber slices. Cut the peel and pith from the lemon, cut out the meaty sections between the membranes, and slice these sections into wafer-thin triangles; arrange these lemon triangles on top of the salmon. Place a mound of caviar in the center and sprigs of dill around the outer edge of each serving.

Field Salad with Tart Apple and Champagne Vinaigrette

2 to 3 cups mixed field greens
(such as mâche, arugula, mizuna, Bibb, romaine)
Champagne Vinaigrette (recipe follows)
½ Granny Smith apple, peeled, cored,
and cut into ½-inch dice

Tear the lettuce leaves into pieces and toss with three fourths of the vinaigrette; toss the diced apple with the remaining vinaigrette. Place the tossed greens on 2 salad plates and sprinkle with the diced apple.

Champagne Vinaigrette

¼ cup extra virgin olive oil
1 tablespoon champagne vinegar
1 shallot, minced
Salt and freshly ground white pepper to taste
1 tablespoon minced fresh chervil or parsley

In a small bowl, whisk all the vinaigrette ingredients together.

Fillet of Black Angus Beef with
a Raisin, Pepper, and Armagnac Sauce

Saffron Potatoes

2 cups Chicken Stock (page 220) or canned chicken broth
Pinch of saffron
6 small new potatoes, scrubbed

In a medium saucepan, bring the chicken stock or broth to a boil, then add the saffron. Remove the pan from heat and let steep for 5 minutes. Return the pan to heat and bring the stock to a boil. Add the potatoes and cook for about 15 minutes, or until potatoes are tender when pierced with a knife.

Steamed Spinach

1 small bunch spinach, stemmed
Salt and pepper to taste

Wash the spinach and place it, still wet, in a large covered pan. Cook 3 to 4 minutes over high heat until wilted. Place in a sieve and press with the back of a large spoon to drain excess liquid.

Fillets with Raisin, Pepper, and Armagnac Sauce

¼ cup seedless yellow raisins
1 cup boiling water
3 tablespoons Armagnac
1 tablespoon peppercorns
Two 8-ounce Black Angus tenderloin steaks
1 teaspoon coarse salt
2 tablespoons butter
⅓ cup Veal Stock (page 226) or reduced canned chicken broth
Salt and pepper to taste

In a small bowl, soak the raisins in the boiling water for 5 minutes; drain. Add 2 tablespoons of the Armagnac to the raisins and set aside.

Spread the peppercorns on top of waxed paper on a flat work surface, and crush them with a rolling pin. Sprinkle the steaks with the salt and roll them in the crushed peppercorns. In a sauté pan or skillet, melt 1 tablespoon of the butter over medium-high heat and cook the steaks for 3 minutes on each side, turning once. Remove from heat and cover with aluminum foil. Reserve the pan and juices for the Armagnac sauce.

Deglaze the pan with the remaining 1 tablespoon of the Armagnac. Add the raisins and their liquid, and cook over medium heat to reduce the liquid by one half. Add the veal stock or chicken broth and reduce again by one half. Fold in the remaining 1 tablespoon of butter, stirring continually, and continue cooking until the sauce thickens enough to coat the back of a spoon. Season with salt and pepper.

Serving. Immediately place a portion of warm spinach in the center of each of 2 dinner plates. Top each with a steak and spoon some of the sauce over. Surround with saffron potatoes and steamed baby vegetables of your choice. Serve at once.

Praline and Armagnac Mousse
with Caramel Sauce

Caramel Sauce

½ cup sugar
2 tablespoons cold water
¼ cup hot water
1 tablespoon Armagnac

In a small heavy saucepan, bring the sugar and cold water to a boil over medium heat, stirring to dissolve the sugar. Cook the syrup over a low heat until it is a rich golden brown, watching carefully to see that it does not burn; then remove it from the heat. Holding the pan away from you, add the hot water, swirling the pan to incorporate the water into the caramel. Return to the heat and simmer for 1 minute; remove from the heat and add the Armagnac. Let cool. Refrigerated in a covered container, this sauce will keep for weeks.

Praline and Armagnac Mousse

2 tablespoons cold water
6 tablespoons sugar
2 tablespoons hot water
2 egg yolks
2 tablespoon superfine sugar
½ cup heavy (whipping) cream
1 ounce (1 square) semisweet chocolate
½ tablespoon Armagnac

In a small, heavy saucepan, combine the cold water and sugar and bring to a boil over medium heat, stirring to dissolve the sugar. Reduce to low and cook until the caramel turns golden brown. Remove from the heat and, holding the pan away from you, add the hot water, swirling the pan to blend.

In a medium bowl, beat the egg yolks and the superfine sugar with an electric mixer until the mixture thickens enough to form ribbons when the beaters are lifted. Reduce the speed to medium and gradually pour in the hot caramel; continue beating until the mixture cools.

In a deep bowl, whip the cream until it forms soft peaks. In the top of a double boiler, melt the chocolate. Remove the chocolate from the heat and stir in 2 tablespoons of the whipped cream, then fold the chocolate mixture into the remaining whipped cream. Add the Armagnac. Fold the chocolate mixture into the caramel mixture, stirring until fully blended.

Fill two 4-inch ramekins with the mousse mixture, smoothing the top with a spatula. Freeze for at least 4 hours.

Garnish

2 tablepoons sliced almonds
2 tablespoons sugar
2 tablespoons kirsch

Just before serving, preheat the oven to 400° F. In a small bowl, combine the sliced almonds, sugar, and kirsch. Spread this mixture on a baking sheet and bake in the preheated oven for about 5 minutes, until golden brown.

Serving. Briefly dip the ramekins in hot water and unmold onto the center of 2 chilled dessert plates. Spoon caramel sauce over the mousse and garnish with toasted almonds.

FEARRINGTON HOUSE

Pittsboro, North Carolina

The Fearrington farm has been part of the pastoral landscape between Chapel Hill and Pittsboro, North Carolina, for two centuries. The dairy barn and silo still dominate the landscape, and cows still graze in the meadow. R.B. and Jenny Fitch bought the six-hundred-acre farm and have realized a dream by creating a country village that today includes homes, shops, and a market. At the center of the village is The Fearrington House, a restaurant and fourteen-room country inn with membership in Relais & Chateaux and a Four-Diamond Award from the American Automobile Association.

The inspiration to add overnight accommodations to The Fearrington House came from the Fitches' experiences in European country inns. Adjacent to the original home, the Inn is clustered around a lovely courtyard. The rooms and suites are individually decorated with English antiques and original art. Guests at the Inn enjoy bicycle rides to the Swim and Croquet Club, strolls to the village, flowering gardens, and the finest of Southern hospitality.

The family home, built in 1927, has become The Fearrington House Restaurant, which is a collection of small dining rooms. Its sophisticated Southern cuisine, prepared with classical techniques, has made it one of the great restaurants of the American South. The restaurant's wine list has received the *Wine Spectator's* Award of Excellence as one of the most outstanding wine lists in the world. Jenny Fitch, the inspiration and guiding spirit behind the restaurant, has created the following dinner for two and presented it to *Menus and Music*.

The Fearrington House

THE MENU

The Fearrington House

Raspberry Kir

Asparagus Vinaigrette

Red Snapper with Matchstick Vegetables

Lemon Rice with Almonds

Glazed Baby Carrots

Fresh Fruit with Grand Marnier Sauce

Raspberry Kir

¼ cup defrosted frozen raspberries
2 tablespoons Grand Marnier
1 split (7 ounces) of champagne

Strain the raspberries through a sieve to remove the seeds. Add the Grand Marnier and chill.

Place 1½ teaspoons of the raspberry mixture in the bottom of each of 2 champagne flutes. Slowly fill with champagne and serve immediately.

The Fearrington House

Asparagus Vinaigrette

1 tablespoon Tarragon Vinegar (recipe follows)
⅛ teaspoon salt
1 teaspoon Dijon mustard
3 tablespoons Basil-Garlic Olive Oil (recipe follows)
Freshly ground pepper to taste
12 asparagus spears
1 hard-boiled egg
Lettuce leaves
¼ red bell pepper, cored, seeded, and minced
1 tablespoon chopped fresh chives, tarragon, chervil, and/or parsley

In a wooden bowl, combine the vinegar and salt and whisk until the salt dissolves. Add the mustard and then slowly whisk the basil-garlic olive oil into the mixture by the spoonful. As the mustard absorbs the oil, the dressing will become thick and emulsified. Add freshly ground pepper to taste and set aside.

Snap the ends off the asparagus spears, then wash and drain. Boil the asparagus for about 2 minutes, or until the spears can be pierced with a fork but are still crunchy. Drain and immediately plunge the asparagus into cold water to set the bright green color; set aside.

Push the hard-boiled egg through a sieve with a spoon.

Serving. Line 2 plates with lettuce leaves and divide the asparagus spears between them. Drizzle with the vinaigrette. Garnish with the sieved egg and red bell pepper. Sprinkle the herbs on top.

The Fearrington House

Tarragon Vinegar

Three 4-inch tarragon sprigs
1 cup white wine vinegar, heated

Place the tarragon sprigs in a half-pint glass container. Using a funnel, fill the container with the hot white wine vinegar. Seal it and set it aside in a dark, cool place for at least a month for the flavors to develop.

Basil-Garlic Olive Oil

2 to 3 garlic cloves
3 basil sprigs
1 cup good-quality olive oil

Skewer the garlic cloves on a toothpick and place it in the bottom of a half-pint glass container. Push the basil into the jar and add the olive oil. Set in a dark place for a couple of months to let the flavors develop. Strain through double layers of cheesecloth or a fine sieve before use.

The Fearrington House

Red Snapper with Matchstick Vegetables

2 teaspoons butter
One 8-ounce red snapper fillet
Salt and pepper to taste
1 shallot, minced
4 lemon thyme sprigs
½ cup mixed matchstick-cut vegetables
(yellow squash, zucchini, and red bell pepper)
About 10 snow peas, cut into diagonal pieces
2 tablespoons dry white wine
2 lemon slices

Preheat the oven to 400° F. On a clean work surface, lay out two 9-by-12-inch pieces of parchment. Cut 1 teaspoon of the butter into thin shavings and place half in the center of the narrow end of each piece of parchment. Cut the fish in half and place each piece on top of the butter, skin side down. Sprinkle the salt, pepper, shallot, and lemon thyme over the fish. Surround the fish with matchstick vegetables and snow peas. Pour 1 tablespoon of wine over each piece of fish and top with a lemon slice.

Completely enclose each piece of fish in parchment by loosely rolling the paper. Fold the ends of each packet, and use the strings to tie both ends shut to resemble a handle. Make sure the paper is not torn. Place the packets in a baking pan and bake in the preheated oven for 15 to 20 minutes. Transfer to a warm platter and cut the packets open just before serving.

Lemon Rice with Almonds

1 teaspoon butter
3 tablespoons minced onion
½ cup long-grain rice
1 cup Chicken Stock (page 220) or canned chicken broth
2 tablespoons fresh lemon juice
1 teaspoon grated lemon zest (page 86)
2 tablespoons slivered blanched almonds, lightly toasted*

In a sauté pan or skillet, melt the butter and sauté the onion for about 5 minutes, or until translucent but not browned. Blend in the rice and stir until all the grains are coated. Add the chicken broth, lemon juice, and lemon zest. Bring to a boil, lower the heat and simmer, covered, for about 20 minutes, or until all the liquid is absorbed. Remove from the heat, blend in the almonds, and serve.

*To toast almonds, spread blanched (skinless) almonds in a jelly-roll pan and toast until light brown (about 10 minutes) in a preheated 350° F oven, tossing several times. To make ahead of time; cool thoroughly, pack the nuts into a covered container, and freeze.

The Fearrington House

Glazed Baby Carrots

6 baby carrots
¼ cup brown sugar
1 tablespoon orange juice
1 tablespoon grated orange zest (page 86)
½ cup water
1 teaspoon butter

Peel the carrots and leave ½ inch of the green top attached. In a saucepan or skillet, cook the carrots in water to cover for 5 to 8 minutes, or until crisp-tender. Drain and set aside.

In a small saucepan, combine the brown sugar, orange juice, orange zest, and water. Bring to a boil and add the butter. Cook until the liquid is thickened and reduced and the sugar is dissolved. Add the carrots, coat them with the glaze, heat through, and serve.

The Fearrington House

Fresh Fruit with Grand Marnier Sauce

¼ cup sugar
¾ cup water
1 teaspoon fresh lemon juice
1 teaspoon Grand Marnier
1 orange, peeled
1 kiwi, peeled
6 strawberries, stemmed
About 10 seedless green grapes, stemmed
¼ cup blueberries, stemmed
Grand Marnier Sauce (recipe follows)

In a small saucepan, make a simple syrup by dissolving the sugar in the water at a simmer, stirring constantly. Remove from the heat and let cool. Add the lemon juice and Grand Marnier, and set aside.

Slice the orange, kiwi, and strawberries into crosswise pieces. Cut the grapes in half. Add all the fruit to the syrup, combine thoroughly, and chill.

Serving. Spoon the fruit into 2 dessert bowls or goblets and top with Grand Marnier sauce. Serve with cookies (try the Almond Cookies on page 208).

Grand Marnier Sauce

2 egg yolks
2 tablespoons sugar
½ cup heavy (whipping) cream
1 tablespoon Grand Marnier

Place the egg yolks and sugar in the top of a double boiler or over very low heat. Cook slowly, stirring constantly for about 10 minutes, or until the sugar has dissolved and the mixture has thickened enough to coat the back of a spoon.

The Fearrington House

The slow cooking process is important, for it allows the eggs to cook without scrambling. If the spoon picks up clumps from the bottom of the pan, the temperature is too hot. Set aside to cool.

In a deep bowl, whip the cream until soft peaks form when the beater is lifted. Combine the cream with the yolk mixture and Grand Marnier.

Makes about 1 cup

HASTINGS HOUSE

Ganges, British Columbia

Hastings House is an award-winning seaside resort in an idyllic setting on Salt Spring Island. Donald Cross purchased a small residential farm from Warren Hastings and has transformed the property into a tranquil country hotel. The five buildings on the estate have been thoughtfully restored with charming accommodations and public rooms. The Tudor-style Manor House, seasoned by character and tradition, has an atmosphere of casual elegance and complete relaxation, and all the comfortably decorated guest suites have wood-burning fireplaces. The thirty acres of gentle pasture, quiet forest, and shoreline that make up the Hastings House grounds are perfect for wandering. Photographers, artists, and nature lovers will treasure the abundance of wildlife on the property. Cycling is popular on the island and a golf course and tennis courts are in the vicinity of the resort.

The cuisine offered in the Manor House dining room features produce and herbs from the garden, eggs from the hen house, and fruit from trees and bushes on the estate. Salt Spring lamb and local seafood are featured regularly. Hastings House guests are presented at the table with a hand-calligraphed menu inscribed with their name. Chef Geoffrey Couper created the following dinner for two for *Menus and Music*.

THE MENU

Hastings House

*Ribbons of Smoked Salmon with
Warm Potato Pancakes and Dill Cream*

Roast Carrot and Lobster Bisque

*Rack of Lamb on an Onion and
Chèvre Compote with Morel Sauce*

*Poached Pears with
Caramel Sauce and Toasted Hazelnuts*

Ribbons of Smoked Salmon with
Warm Potato Pancakes and Dill Cream

1 cup peeled finely grated raw potato
2 tablespoons minced onion
1 teaspoon grated lemon zest (page 86)
2 tablespoons flour
1 egg
¼ cup heavy (whipping) cream
1 teaspoon chopped fresh parsley
Pinch of grated nutmeg
Salt and pepper to taste
2 tablespoons butter
2 ounces smoked salmon, thinly sliced and chilled
Dill Cream (recipe follows)
Salmon and sturgeon caviar for garnish
Fresh dill sprigs for garnish
Freshly ground pepper to taste

Preheat the oven to 350° F. In a mixing bowl, combine the potato, onion, lemon zest, flour, egg, cream, parsley, nutmeg, salt, and pepper. In a sauté pan or skillet, melt 1 tablespoon of the butter over medium heat and add one half of the pancake mixture. Flatten the pancake with a spatula and cook until lightly browned. Flip the pancake over, lightly brown, then set aside in a shallow baking pan. Repeat the process with the remaining potato mixture. Place the second pancake in the baking pan and place the pan in the preheated oven for 10 minutes to finish cooking.

Serving. Cut each potato pancake into 6 wedges and arrange them attractively on a serving plate. Decorate the pancakes with ribbons of smoked salmon and top with a dollop of dill cream. Garnish with the caviar and dill sprigs. Grind black pepper over each pancake and serve immediately.

Hastings House

Dill Cream

¼ cup Crème Fraîche (page 221) or sour cream
2 teaspoons chopped fresh dill
Fresh lemon juice, salt, and white pepper to taste

In a mixing bowl, whisk together the crème fraîche, dill, lemon juice, salt, and pepper until thoroughly blended. Cover and chill.

Hastings House

Roast Carrot and Lobster Bisque

4 teaspoons butter
1 ¼ cups diced peeled carrots
¼ cup minced onions
1 tablespoon flour
3 cups Lobster Stock (recipe follows)
Salt, white pepper, and cayenne pepper to taste
Lobster meat, diced
Crème Fraîche (page 221) or sour cream for garnish
Chervil sprigs for garnish

Preheat the oven to 400° F. In an ovenproof sauté pan or skillet, melt the butter over medium-high heat and sauté the diced carrots and minced onions until soft. Cover the pan, place it in the preheated oven and roast for 30 to 40 minutes, stirring occasionally. Remove from the oven and sprinkle the flour over the vegetables, stirring well. Slowly add the lobster stock and simmer the bisque for 5 minutes. Remove from the stove and purée the bisque in a blender or food processor. Adjust the seasoning.

Serving. Ladle the bisque into 2 serving bowls. Garnish with the diced lobster meat, a dollop of crème fraîche, and chervil sprigs.

Lobster Stock

1 onion, thinly sliced (about ¾ cup)
1 carrot, peeled and sliced (about ½ cup)
2 celery stalks, sliced (about ½ cup)
3 tablespoons butter
10 white peppercorns
2 thyme sprigs
2 bay leaves
10 cups cold water
One 1-pound live lobster
1 tablespoon tomato paste

In a large stockpot, sauté half of the onion, carrot, and celery in 1½ tablespoons of the butter until soft. Add the peppercorns, herbs, and cold water. Cover and bring to a rapid boil. Plunge the lobster into the boiling liquid, return to boiling, and cook for 9 minutes. Remove the lobster from the boiling liquid with a slotted spoon and let cool. Reserve the cooking liquid.

Shell the lobster and reserve the shells. Dice the lobster meat and set aside. In a large skillet, melt the remaining 1½ tablespoons butter over medium-high heat and sauté the remaining sliced onion, celery, and carrot until soft. Add the tomato paste, reserved lobster shells, and cooking liquid. Bring to a slow boil and reduce to about 3 cups. Strain the stock through a sieve and set aside.

Hastings House

Rack of Lamb on a White Onion and
Chèvre Compote with Morel Sauce

Morel Sauce

1 tablespoon dried morels
1 tablespoon finely diced shallots
3 tablespoons dry white wine
¾ cup strong Lamb Stock (page 224) or reduced canned chicken broth
2 tablespoons cold butter, cut into half-inch pieces
Salt and freshly ground black pepper to taste

Soak the morels in warm water for 30 minutes. Strain the soaking liquid though a coffee filter and reserve the liquid. Cut the morels crosswise into rings and wash thoroughly until all sand is removed. In a sauté pan or skillet, melt 1 tablespoon of the butter and sauté the shallots slowly; add the morels, cover, and simmer for 10 minutes. Add the white wine, the reserved soaking liquid, and the lamb stock or chicken broth and reduce by two thirds. Over low heat, swirl in the remaining butter pieces and adjust the final seasoning with salt and pepper.

Potatoes Dauphinoise

2 potatoes, peeled and thinly sliced
2 tablespoons butter
¼ cup grated Gruyère or Parmesan cheese
Salt and pepper to taste

Preheat the oven to 350° F. Butter a baking dish and arrange a layer of potatoes in the bottom. Dot with half the butter and sprinkle with half the grated cheese, and sprinkle with salt and pepper. Repeat with a second layer of potatoes, top with the remaining butter and cheese, and sprinkle with salt and pepper. Cover the baking dish with aluminum foil and bake in the preheated oven until the potatoes are tender, about 1 hour.

Lamb

One 8-bone rack of lamb, Frenched and trimmed of fat
2 tablespoons olive oil
Freshly ground pepper
1 tablespoon vegetable oil

Remove the lamb from the refrigerator 45 minutes before roasting to bring it to room temperature. Preheat the oven to 425° F. Rub the lamb with the olive oil and season it with pepper. In a large ovenproof skillet, heat the vegetable oil to almost smoking and quickly brown the lamb on all sides. Place the skillet in the preheated oven and roast for 12 to 15 minutes, or until the lamb is medium rare, or to your preference. Remove the roasting pan from the oven and let the lamb sit for 10 minutes before carving.

Onion and Chèvre Compote

1 tablespoon butter
⅔ cup finely diced onion
4 teaspoons minced garlic
2 tablespoons dry white wine
1 tablespoon white wine vinegar
½ cup heavy (whipping) cream
¼ cup fresh chèvre, coarsely diced
2 teaspoons minced fresh parsley and chives
Salt and freshly ground white pepper to taste

Hastings House

In a medium, heavy saucepan, melt the butter over medium heat and sauté the onion and garlic for 2 minutes, or until translucent. Add the white wine, reduce the heat to low, cover, and slowly stew for 10 minutes, stirring occasionally. Add the vinegar and cream, increase the heat to medium, and allow to reduce until it is thick enough to coat the back of a spoon. Shortly before serving, fold in the chèvre, parsley, chives, salt, and pepper, and heat through.

Vegetables

1 bunch asparagus, trimmed
1 bunch baby carrots, trimmed

Cook the asparagus and carrots separately in simmering water to cover for 3 to 5 minutes, or until crisp-tender.

Serving. Slicing closely against the rib bones, remove the loin from the rack. Divide the rack in half to use as a base for the sliced loin. Slice the loin into about 10 slices. Divide the onion and chèvre compote evenly between 2 warm dinner plates. Place 4 rib racks to one side of the compote on each plate and lay the loin slices over. Ladle the morel sauce around the compote. Serve with the fresh asparagus, baby carrots, and potatoes dauphinoise.

Poached Pears with
Caramel Sauce and Toasted Hazelnuts

¾ cup sugar
2 cups water
2 Bosc pears, peeled, halved, and cored
Caramel Sauce (recipe follows)
4 teaspoons toasted hazelnuts (page 225), chopped
Powdered sugar and mint sprigs

In a medium saucepan, bring the sugar and water to a simmer over medium heat, stirring until the sugar just dissolves; remove from heat. Place the pear halves in the saucepan with the sugar syrup right after peeling them in order to prevent discoloration. Poach the pears over low heat and keep just below a simmer; actual simmering will burst the fruit. Poach the pears until tender when pierced with a sharp knife, about 10 minutes.

Remove the pan from the heat and let the pears cool in the syrup. Remove the pear halves with a slotted spoon, and cut each pear lengthwise into 3 wedges; set aside.

Serving. Divide the poached pear wedges between 2 serving plates. Spoon the caramel sauce over the pears and garnish with toasted hazelnuts, powdered sugar, and mint sprigs.

Note: The pears can be cooked several days in advance and refrigerated in their poaching liquid.

Hastings House

Caramel Sauce

½ cup plus 4 teaspoons sugar
½ vanilla bean, split lengthwise
1 cup milk
4 egg yolks
4 teaspoons Frangelica (hazelnut) liqueur
½ cup heavy (whipping) cream

In a heavy saucepan, place ½ cup of the sugar and the vanilla bean. Cook over medium heat until the sugar turns a light caramel brown. Reduce the heat and pour in the milk; slowly bring to a simmer. Remove the vanilla bean with a slotted spoon, then scrape the vanilla seeds back into the milk mixture.

In a small bowl, whisk together the egg yolks and the remaining 4 teaspoons of sugar. Add one third of the warm milk mixture to the eggs, blending well. Pour this egg mixture back into the milk mixture and cook slowly, being very careful not to boil. Stir constantly until the sauce has thickened enough to coat the back of a spoon.

Remove this light custard from the heat and set the pan in a bowl of ice water until well chilled. Stir in the Frangelica liqueur. Refrigerated in a covered container, this sauce will keep for weeks. Just before serving, in a deep bowl whip the cream until it forms stiff peaks, and fold it into the caramel sauce.

Hastings House

THE HOME RANCH

Clark, Colorado

The Home Ranch is set on the northern end of the beautiful Elk River Valley in Clark, Colorado. Kendrick Jones is the builder and owner of this peaceful Rocky Mountain hideaway, which offers a gracious combination of western warmth, creature comforts, and lively outdoor activity. The Home Ranch is a member of Relais & Chateaux.

In winter, The Home Ranch offers spectacular cross-country skiing on groomed trails throughout the Elk River Valley, snowshoeing, and sleigh rides. There is downhill skiing and shopping at nearby Steamboat Springs. In summer, horseback riding is very popular and is suited to every level of skill, from kids' rides to roping and barrel racing. Guests enjoy fishing in the Ranch's trout-stocked pond or the Elk River, hiking, and llama trekking. A sauna and a lap pool add to the luxury of this mountain retreat.

The Home Ranch's seven private guest cabins are furnished with antiques, Indian rugs, and original artwork. A Jacuzzi on each cabin porch is especially welcome after a day of riding, hiking, or skiing. Dinners of gourmet western fare are served in the Main House. The Home Ranch chef Clyde Nelson created the following dinner for two for *Menus and Music*.

THE MENU

The Home Ranch

*Cream of Sunchoke Soup with
Cilantro Cream and Potato Biscuits*

*Spinach Salad with Achiote Grilled Shrimp,
Eggplant, and Roasted Red Pepper*

Stuffed Pheasant Breast with Sun-dried Berry Sauce

Wild and Brown Rice with Apple and Pecans

Buttered Asparagus

Chocolate Crêpes with Mascarpone and Blood Orange Sauce

Cream of Sunchoke Soup with
Cilantro Cream and Potato Biscuits

Cream of Sunchoke Soup

5 tablespoons butter

½ cup chopped onions

1 stalk celery, chopped

½ leek (white part and 1 inch of green), diced

¼ pound sunchokes (Jerusalem artichokes), peeled and chopped

¼ cup unbleached all-purpose flour

5 cups Chicken Stock (page 220) or canned chicken broth

*Several parsley stems, 1 bay leaf, 3 or 4 peppercorns,
and 2 or 3 thyme sprigs, tied in a square of cheesecloth*

1 cup heavy (whipping) cream

Salt and pepper to taste

In a heavy 2-quart pot, melt the butter over medium heat. Add the onions, celery, and leek; cover and cook slowly for 10 minutes, or until onions are translucent. Add the sunchokes and flour, and cook slowly for another 2 to 3 minutes. Whisk the chicken stock or broth into the vegetables. Add the bag of herbs. Bring the liquid to a simmer and cook until the vegetables are tender, about 20 minutes. Remove the pot from the heat and remove the bouquet with a slotted spoon. In a food processor or blender, purée the soup until smooth. Add the cream and adjust the seasoning with salt and pepper.

61

Cilantro Cream

½ bunch watercress, or 3 leaves spinach, blanched and pressed dry
½ cup fresh cilantro leaves
2 tablespoons Crème Fraîche (page 221) or sour cream
Salt and pepper to taste

In a blender or food processor, purée the cilantro and watercress with 2 to 3 tablespoons of the crème frâiche until smooth. Strain through a sieve into a small bowl and stir in the remaining crème frâiche. Adjust the seasoning with salt and pepper and refrigerate covered until needed.

Makes about 1 cup

Potato Biscuits

This is a three-day project.

8 ounces baking potatoes, unpeeled
1 package (2 teaspoons) active dry yeast
1½ tablespoons warm (105° to 115° F) water
2 cups unbleached bread flour
1 teaspoon salt
1 cup (2 sticks) cold butter
1 egg yolk, beaten with 1 tablespoon cold water

In a saucepan, boil the potatoes in water to cover until tender when pierced by a sharp knife. Cool completely, peel, and roughly chop. Dissolve the yeast in the warm water and let sit for 10 minutes. In a food processor, combine the flour and salt. Cut in the butter by pulsing the processor 8 or 9 times, then add the potatoes. Process briefly until you have a soft dough. Or, in a large bowl, combine the flour and salt; cut in the butter with a pastry cutter or 2 knives. Add the potatoes and stir with a wooden spoon until you have a soft dough.

Remove the dough to a floured work surface, pat out, and shape the dough into a 8-by-12-inch rectangle. Fold in thirds as you would a letter. Cover loosely and chill for 2 hours. Remove from refrigerator and roll out again into an 8-by-12-inch rectangle. Fold again into thirds and chill for 24 hours. Roll out, fold again, and chill for 2 more hours.

Roll out the dough into a 9-by-15-inch rectangle about ½ inch thick. With a sharp knife, cut the dough into forty-five 1-by-3-inch rectangles. (Make 8 lengthwise cuts, 1 inch apart, and 4 crosswise cuts, 3 inches apart.) Place them on a lightly greased baking sheet. Let rise for 20 to 25 minutes. Meanwhile, preheat the oven to 400° F. Brush the biscuits with the egg wash and bake for 16 to 18 minutes, or until golden.

After the biscuits have completely cooled, you may freeze the extras for another time.

Makes 45 biscuits

Finishing the Soup

4 poached artichoke bottoms (page 159)

Quarter the artichoke bottoms. Add them to the soup and heat for several minutes.

Serving. Ladle the soup into 2 bowls and swirl the cilantro cream on top. Serve with potato biscuits.

Spinach Salad with Achiote Grilled Shrimp, Eggplant, and Roasted Red Pepper

1 red bell pepper
8 large shrimp
1 tablespoon achiote paste*
Orange juice to cover the shrimp
¼ cup peeled and cubed eggplant
1 tablespoon olive oil
3 cups washed and stemmed spinach leaves
4 sun-dried tomatoes, chopped
4 mushrooms, sliced
½ cup Garlic Vinaigrette (recipe follows)
1 hard-boiled egg, pushed through a sieve
1 tablespoon pine nuts, toasted**

Light a charcoal fire in an open grill. When the fire is red hot, roast the red pepper on the grill, turning it to blacken all over. Remove the pepper from the grill, place it in a paper bag, and close it tightly. When the pepper is cool, after about 15 minutes, remove its skin, core, and seeds. Slice the pepper into thin strips and set aside.

In a ceramic bowl, stir together the achiote paste and enough orange juice to cover the shrimp. Marinate the shrimp in this liquid in the refrigerator for 20 minutes. Grill the shrimp for a minute or so on each side, and set aside.

In a sauté pan or skillet, sauté the eggplant cubes in the olive oil until soft and let cool. In a large bowl, combine the spinach, sun-dried tomatoes, eggplant, and mushrooms. Pour ¼ cup of the garlic vinaigrette into the bowl and toss with the vegetables.

Serving. Divide the spinach, tomatoes, eggplant and mushrooms between 2 plates. Arrange the red pepper on top and surround with the shrimp. Garnish with the sieved egg and pine nuts. Pour some of the remaining garlic vinaigrette on top.

The Home Ranch

*Achiote paste may be found in Latino markets.

** In a small dry skillet over medium heat, toast the pine nuts, stirring, for several minutes until lightly browned.

Garlic Vinaigrette

¼ cup olive oil
⅓ cup corn oil
¼ cup white wine vinegar
½ teaspoon salt
½ teaspoon freshly ground black pepper
½ tablespoon minced garlic
1 teaspoon chopped fresh basil, or ½ teaspoon dried basil
1 teaspoon chopped fresh oregano, or ½ teaspoon dried oregano
¼ cup minced fresh parsley

Whisk together all the ingredients. Store in the refrigerator and use for salads.

Makes about 1 cup

Stuffed Pheasant Breast with Sun-dried Berry Sauce

One 3-pound pheasant or chicken

Remove each breast from the pheasant or chicken, carefully keeping the wingbone attached and the skin intact. Remove the legs and thighs from the carcass. Remove the meat from the thighs and set aside for stuffing. Set aside the carcass and legs for the glace.

Pheasant Stuffing

8 ounces pheasant thigh meat
2 tablespoons crushed ice
Salt and white pepper to taste
⅓ cup heavy (whipping) cream
1 teaspoon minced fresh sage, or ¼ teaspoon dried sage
1 tablespoon smoked ham
(Westphalian or Black Forest), finely diced

In a blender or food processor, place the thigh meat, crushed ice, salt, and pepper. Process for 1 minute. With the motor running, slowly pour in the cream and purée. Remove to a bowl and fold in the sage and ham. Cover and chill at least 1 hour in the refrigerator.

Flatten each breast gently with the flat of a large knife. Starting at the narrow part, gently slide your fingers between the flesh and skin and slightly lift the skin away to expose the flesh. Wet your fingers in cold water and place 2 to 3 tablespoons of stuffing under the skin of each breast, tapering the layer at the edges. Pull the skin back over the filling and tuck any excess under the edges of the breast. Place the breasts between waxed paper and chill until ready to use.

The Home Ranch

Pheasant Glace

2 tablespoons oil

Carcass and leg bones from pheasant or chicken, coarsely chopped

1 small carrot, peeled and finely diced

½ medium onion, finely diced

2 shallots, finely diced

6 juniper berries

2 to 3 thyme sprigs, or ½ teaspoon dried thyme

1 bay leaf

½ cup dry white wine

2 cups Veal Stock (page 226) or reduced canned chicken broth

1 tablespoon bourbon

Salt and pepper to taste

In a heavy 2-quart pot, heat the oil. When very hot, add the carcass and bones. Brown the bones slowly for 15 to 20 minutes. Stir in the carrot, onion, and shallots and slowly brown them for another 5 minutes. Add the juniper berries, thyme, bay leaf, and white wine. Boil to reduce by two thirds. Add the stock or broth and bourbon. Simmer gently for 30 to 45 minutes. Remove from heat and strain through a sieve. Pour the liquid back into a pot and boil to reduce to ½ cup. Season with salt and pepper and set aside.

Sun-dried Berry Sauce

¼ cup mixed sun-dried cherries, cranberries, and blueberries

½ cup port wine

1 shallot, minced

1 serrano chili, minced

In saucepan, combine the dried berries, port wine, shallot, and chili. Cook until the berries are soft and the liquid has reduced to a syrup. Set aside.

Cooking and Garnishing the Pheasant

Salt and pepper to taste
Flour for dredging
Prepared stuffed pheasant or chicken breasts
2 tablespoons clarified butter (page 220)
¼ cup black currant or raspberry vinegar
¼ cup bourbon
⅓ cup Pheasant Glace
Prepared berry syrup
1 tablespoon butter
Mint or sage sprigs for garnish

Preheat the oven to 375° F. Season the pheasant or chicken breasts and dredge them in flour, then shake off the excess. In an ovenproof sauté pan or skillet, heat the butter to medium-hot. Place the breasts in the pan skin side down and sauté until golden brown. Turn over and sear for 2 to 3 more minutes. Drape the breasts lightly with parchment paper or buttered aluminum foil and place the pan in the preheated oven. Roast for approximately 15 to 20 minutes, or until the juices run clear when the meat is pierced with a knife at the wing joint. Remove the breasts from the pan and keep warm on a serving platter.

Deglaze the roasting pan with the vinegar and bourbon over medium heat. Reduce the liquid by one half, then add the pheasant glace and reduce again until syrupy. Add the berry syrup. Swirl in the tablespoon of butter.

Serving. Ladle the sauce onto 2 plates. Place the breasts on top and garnish with fresh mint or sage. Serve immediately.

The Home Ranch

Wild and Brown Rice with Apple and Pecans

1 tablespoon corn oil
1 tablespoon butter
¼ cup minced onion
1 celery stalk, minced
1 garlic clove, minced
½ cup wild rice
¼ cup brown rice
1 ½ cups hot Chicken Stock (page 220) or canned chicken broth
¼ cup chopped peeled apple
¼ cup toasted pecans,* chopped
2 tablespoons minced fresh parsley
Salt and pepper to taste

In a medium saucepan, heat the oil and butter over medium-high heat. Add the onion, celery, and garlic and sauté over low heat until the onion is translucent. Add the wild and brown rice and stir. Cook for 30 seconds. Add the hot chicken stock or broth, tightly cover the pan, and simmer over low heat for 40 minutes. Stir in the apple and pecans and cover again. Simmer another 10 minutes, or until the rice is tender. Add additional stock or broth if necessary. Stir in the parsley, salt, and pepper.

*To toast pecans, spread on a jelly-roll pan or baking sheet and toast until light brown (about 10 minutes) in a preheated 350° F oven, tossing several times.

The Home Ranch

Buttered Asparagus

1 quart water
¾ pound young asparagus
2 tablespoons butter
¼ cup Chicken Stock (page 220) or canned chicken broth
Salt and pepper to taste

In a large pot, bring the water to a boil. Meanwhile, prepare the asparagus by breaking off the woody stems and partially peeling the stalks with a vegetable peeler. Boil them until crisp-tender, about 3 to 5 minutes. (The time will depend upon the size of the asparagus.) Remove from the boiling water and submerge in ice cold water. Drain and set aside.

Just before serving, melt the butter in a sauté pan or skillet over medium-high heat. Add the chicken stock or broth and asparagus, and cook until almost all the liquid evaporates. Season with salt and pepper. Divide the asparagus between 2 plates and pour the syrupy butter over them.

Chocolate Crêpes with
Mascarpone and Blood Orange Sauce

Chocolate Crêpes

⅞ cup unbleached all-purpose flour
2 tablespoons cocoa
1 ½ tablespoons sugar
⅛ teaspoon salt
⅞ cup milk combined with ¼ cup water
3 eggs
1 egg yolk
¼ cup clarified butter (page 220)

Sift the flour, cocoa, sugar, and salt into a medium bowl. Stir in the combined milk and water. Beat in the eggs and yolk and then the clarified butter. Beat the batter until smooth. Let rest 1 hour in the refrigerator.

Mascarpone Filling

1 egg yolk
1 tablespoon powdered sugar
¾ tablespoon Grand Marnier
½ teaspoon sweet Marsala
¼ cup Mascarpone*

Beat the yolk and sugar until pale and thick. Beat in the liqueurs and wine. Add the Mascarpone and beat until smooth. Chill for at least 1 hour.

*Mascarpone is a sweet creamy Italian cheese available at cheese shops and some grocery stores.

Blood Orange Sauce

4 tablespoons unsalted butter at room temperature
½ cup powdered sugar
½ tablespoon grated blood orange* zest
¼ cup blood orange juice
¼ cup Grand Marnier

In a small bowl, blend the butter and sugar. Add the zest, orange juice, and Grand Marnier. Mix thoroughly and set aside until ready to use.

*The Home Ranch uses blood oranges for this recipe, but navel oranges may be substituted if blood oranges are out of season or unavailable.

Cooking the Crêpes

clarified butter (page 220)

Heat an 8-inch skillet until medium hot. Ladle 1 teaspoon clarified butter into the pan, swirl, and pour out the excess butter. Stir the crêpe batter. Tilt your pan a little and ladle approximately ⅛ cup of batter into the pan; swirl it around to spread an even paper-thin layer over the bottom of the pan. Cook for about 15 seconds.

Remove the crêpe onto waxed paper and keep warm between 2 plates until ready for use. Repeat the procedure to make 4 crêpes, layering the cooked crêpes on top of each other as you go.

The Home Ranch

Serving and Garnishing

1 tablespoon dark rum
1 blood orange, peeled, cut in sections, and seeded
6 to 8 fresh or frozen raspberries
2 mint sprigs
Sifted powdered sugar for dusting

Spoon 1 tablespoon of Mascarpone filling onto the center of each crêpe. Fold the crêpes in half, then again into quarters. Place 2 crêpes on each of 2 plates and keep warm. Heat the orange sauce and reduce for approximately 5 minutes, or until syrupy. Add the rum, orange sections, and raspberries to the orange sauce. Swirl just enough to warm through and pour over the center of the crêpes. Dust the edges of each crêpe with powdered sugar and garnish with fresh mint.

The Home Ranch

HORIZONS AND COTTAGES

Paget West, Bermuda

Guests at Horizons and Cottages enjoy a stay in old Bermuda while enjoying modern luxury amid timeless natural beauty. The resort is perched on a hilltop in one of Bermuda's oldest and most charming houses and includes eleven secluded guest cottages. The terraced gardens and spacious lawns of the thirty-acre estate overlook Coral Beach and a magnificent expanse of blue sea. Three private tennis courts, a nine-hole golf course, eighteen-hole putting green, and a large freshwater swimming pool offer lively recreation. Guests also can enjoy touring, cycling, and shopping in the nearby town of Hamilton.

The restaurant at Horizons and Cottages serves superb French and Bermudian cuisine and has an outstanding selection of wines. Following a Bermuda tradition, maids cook breakfast en suite and serve it on your private terrace or in your living room. These special morning meals received the 1987 Relais & Chateaux Award for Breakfasts served in rooms outside France. Executive chef E.J. Wiersema created the following menu and recipes for two for *Menus and Music*.

THE MENU

Horizons and Cottages

Flower Zucchini Filled with Chicken Salad

Caviar and Salmon on a Bed of
Aniseed Wild Rice with Vermouth Sauce

Lamb and Veal Fillets on a Rhubarb Compote
with Rosemary Sauce

Baby Beets with Apple and Walnuts

Potatoes Stuffed with Leek Mousse

Baby Carrots in Butter Sauce

Feuillantine of Raspberries

Flower Zucchini Filled with Chicken Salad

Chicken Salad

One 6-ounce chicken breast
1 medium zucchini
1 medium carrot
1 tomato
Fresh grated ginger to taste
Salt and freshly ground pepper to taste

In a saucepan, place the chicken breast in boiling salted water to cover, return to a boil, and skim off any scum that forms. Reduce the heat and simmer for 10 minutes. Remove from the heat and allow the chicken to cool in the liquid. Remove the chicken with a slotted spoon, pull off and discard the skin and bones, dice the meat into small cubes, and place in a medium bowl. Reserve the broth for cooking the carrots and larger zucchini. Cut the zucchini and carrot into cubes the same size as the chicken and blanch them in the reserved chicken broth until crisp-tender. Remove with a slotted spoon and place in the mixing bowl with the chicken. (Reserve the broth for Baby Carrots in Butter Sauce, page 85.) Seed the tomato and cut it into small cubes; add to the diced chicken and vegetables. Stir the fresh ginger into the salad ingredients. Add the raspberry vinaigrette, salt, and pepper.

Note: If you wish to prepare the chicken salad in advance, cover, and chill in the refrigerator for up to 4 hours.

Raspberry Vinaigrette

5 or 6 fresh raspberries
1 tablespoon raspberry vinegar
5 tablespoons soy, safflower, or walnut oil
Salt and pepper to taste

In a blender or a food processor, purée the raspberries until smooth. Slowly add the raspberry vinegar and soya oil and continue blending until smooth. Season with salt and pepper and set aside.

Flower Zucchini

2 flower zucchini (tiny zucchini with flowers still attached)
or pumpkin flowers, or Swiss chard or green cabbage leaves

In a saucepan, blanch the flower zucchini, flowers, or leaves in boiling water for 2 minutes; remove them with a slotted spoon, and quickly chill them in cold water to prevent them from overcooking.

Serving. Carefully open each zucchini flower, fill it with chicken salad, and then close the flower. (Or spread the chicken salad on blanched chard or cabbage leaves and wrap into small packages.) Spoon some raspberry vinaigrette onto each salad plate, and carefully place a zucchini flower, with the zucchini still attached, on top. Slice the zucchini lengthwise, still eeping it attached to the flower, and fan the slices out on the plate.

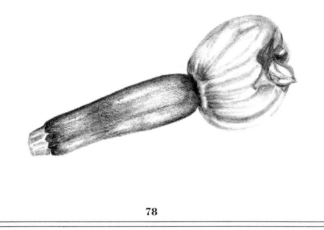

Caviar and Salmon on a Bed of
Aniseed Wild Rice with Vermouth Sauce

Salmon and Caviar

One 8-ounce salmon fillet
1 ounce caviar*
1 egg yolk, beaten

Slice the salmon into 8 thin slices. Using a round pastry cutter with a 3-inch diameter, cut a disk out of each salmon slice. Spoon a dollop of caviar in the middle of each of 4 salmon circles; lightly brush the sides with some egg yolk. Cover the caviar with the remaining 4 salmon circles. Cover and chill.

*Horizons and Cottages uses Beluga caviar, and this is the preferred ingredient.

Aniseed Wild Rice

¼ cup wild rice
1 cup water
⅛ teaspoon salt
Aniseed to taste

Rinse the wild rice thoroughly in cold water and drain. In a heavy saucepan, bring the water to a boil; add the salt and aniseed, and stir in the rice. Return to a boil, reduce heat to a simmer, cover, and cook slowly for 45 minutes to 1 hour, or until the rice is fluffy and the water is absorbed.

Vermouth Sauce

6 tablespoons dry white vermouth*
4 tablespoons Fish Stock (page 222) or clam juice
4 tablespoons minced shallots
1 cup heavy (whipping) cream
Salt and pepper to taste
4 tablespoons butter, melted

In a small saucepan over medium-high heat, cook the vermouth, fish stock or clam juice, and shallots until the liquid is reduced by two thirds. Add the cream and continue cooking until the sauce thickens enough to coat the back of a spoon. Remove from heat and season with salt and pepper. Transfer the sauce to a blender or food processor and purée. Add the butter and blend until smooth.

* Horizons and Cottages uses Noilly Prat vermouth, and this is the preferred ingredient.

Cooking and Garnishing the Salmon

2 tablespoons butter
1 teaspoon minced fresh parsley,
or a few thin slices of fennel bulb for garnish (optional)

In a sauté pan or skillet, melt the butter and fry the salmon for 3 minutes on each side, or until it is opaque, turning carefully.

Serving. Place a portion of rice on each of 2 dinner plates and top with 2 salmon and caviar circles. Cover with warm vermouth sauce and garnish with some parsley or fennel, if you wish.

Lamb and Veal Fillets on a
Rhubarb Compote with Rosemary Sauce

Rhubarb Compote

⅔ pound slender rhubarb stalks

¼ cup water

2 tablespoons honey, or to taste

Salt and pepper to taste

Wash and dry the rhubarb stalks. Trim off the bottom and top of each stalk, including any green, and peel if the skin is tough. Cut the rhubarb into 1-inch pieces. In a covered saucepan, cook the rhubarb, water, and honey over a medium heat for 15 minutes, or until the rhubarb is very soft. Remove from the heat and season with salt and pepper. In a blender or food processor, purée the rhubarb mixture until smooth; set aside.

Rosemary Sauce

2 tablespoons fresh chopped rosemary

4 tablespoons butter

¼ cup minced shallots

2 cups Veal Stock (page 226) or reduced canned chicken broth

Salt and pepper to taste

Using a mortar and pestle, crush the fresh rosemary. In a saucepan, melt 1 tablespoon of the butter and sauté the rosemary and shallots until the shallots are translucent. Add the veal stock or chicken broth and continue cooking until the stock thickens and reduces to half its original volume. Remove from heat and season with salt and pepper. Transfer the sauce to a blender or food processor, add the remaining butter, and purée.

Horizons and Cottages

Lamb and Veal Fillets

1 tablespoon butter
1 teaspoon olive or peanut oil
½ pound veal fillet slices (about ¼ inch thick)
½ pound lamb fillet slices (about ¼ inch thick)
1 small tomato, peeled, seeded, and diced for garnish

Place a sauté pan or skillet over high heat, and film the bottom of the pan with the butter and oil. When the butter begins to foam, add the fillet slices, which should fit in one layer with at least ¼ inch between them. Sauté for about 1½ minutes, turn, and sauté for about 1½ minutes on the other side until medium-rare, or to your own preference.

Serving. Place the rhubarb compote onto 2 plates and lay the veal and lamb fillets on top. Spoon the warm rosemary sauce over the meat and garnish with some diced tomato.

Baby Beets with Apple and Walnuts

4 tiny beets, trimmed and rinsed well
½ apple, peeled and cored
¼ cup walnuts

Place the beets in a small saucepan and add salted water to cover. Bring to a boil, reduce the heat, and simmer until the beets are tender, 20 to 25 minutes. Rinse the beets under cold water, drain, and slip off the skins. To serve, finely chop the apple and walnuts and sprinkle over the cooked beets.

Potatoes Stuffed with Leek Mousse

Leek Mousse (recipe follows)
2 medium potatoes

Prepare the leek mouse. Peel the potatoes and cut away the sides so that each potato is a square block. Scoop out and discard the middle of each potato. Place the potatoes in a pot with enough cold salted water to cover them. Heat the water to boiling, turn down the heat, and gently boil the potatoes until tender when pierced with a knife, about 15 or 20 minutes. Remove the potatoes with a slotted spoon and drain well.

Serving. Warm the leek mouse over low heat. Fill each cooked potato with warm leek mousse and serve with the lamb and veal fillets.

Leek Mousse

1 tablespoon butter
1 leek, minced
⅓ cup heavy (whipping) cream
Salt and pepper to taste

In a sauté pan or skillet, melt the butter and sauté the leek until translucent. Add the cream and reduce until the mousse thickens enough to coat the back of a spoon. Season with salt and pepper.

Horizons and Cottages

Baby Carrots in Butter Sauce

6 baby carrots, peeled
1 cup chicken broth
(use the reserved broth from Flower Zucchini
filled with Chicken Salad, page 77)
⅓ cup dry white wine
Salt and pepper to taste
½ cup (1 stick) butter, cut into cubes

In a saucepan, combine the chicken broth, white wine, salt, and pepper, and cook over high heat to boil down rapidly to a syrup. Remove the pan from the heat and whisk the butter into the broth 2 cubes at a time until creamy. Keep warm over very low heat.

Pour enough salted water in a pot to cover the carrots and heat to boiling. Add the carrots and gently boil until crisp-tender, about 5 to 8 minutes. Drain, coat with some of the butter sauce, and serve.

Horizons and Cottages

Feuillantine of Raspberries

One basket fresh raspberries, or one 10-ounce package
unsweetened frozen raspberries, thawed
2 tablespoons raspberry syrup or framboise
¼ teaspoon grated orange zest*
¼ cup heavy (whipping) cream
Pastry (recipe follows)
Sifted powdered sugar for garnish
2 mint sprigs for garnish

In a small bowl, combine the raspberries, raspberry syrup, and orange zest. In a deep bowl, whip the cream until it forms soft peaks when the beater is lifted. Fill a pastry bag fitted with a round tip with the whipped cream.

Serving. Place a pastry disk on each of 2 plates and pipe the whipped cream along the edges. Spoon the raspberry mixture into the middle of the pastry and cover with a second disk. Sprinkle with powdered sugar and garnish with mint sprigs. Serve immediately.

*For zest, grate the colored part of an orange or lemon peel only; be careful not to grate into the white pith underneath as it is apt to be bitter.

Pastry
¾ cup unbleached all-purpose flour
¾ cup powdered sugar
4 egg whites
½ cup cold clarified butter (page 220)

Horizons and Cottages

In a medium bowl, combine the flour, powdered sugar, and egg whites, mixing until smooth. Stir in the cold but liquid butter, and stir thoroughly. Chill the pastry in the refrigerator for 5 hours before baking.

Preheat the oven to 375° F for at least 20 minutes. Grease a baking sheet. Divide the dough into 4 sections and, using your fingertips, spread the dough into thin round disks 6 inches in diameter. Bake in the preheated oven for 15 to 20 minutes, or until the edges just begin to turn golden. Remove the pastries from the baking sheet with a spatula and let cool. As soon as the pastries are cool, the sugar will set and they will become brittle.

HOTEL HANA-MAUI

Hana, Maui, Hawaii

Guests at the Hotel Hana-Maui experience the unspoiled beauty and traditions of old Hawaii. Hotel Hana-Maui is secluded on the forty-five-hundred-acre Hana Ranch, which lies between the slopes of the ten-thousand-foot Haleakala Volcano, and the dramatic Pacific coastline on the eastern tip of the Hawaiian island of Maui.

Hotel Hana-Maui's strikingly beautiful main lodge and collection of one-story bungalows are tucked amid sixty-six acres of lush tropical gardens. The architecture of the recently completed Sea Ranch cottages was inspired by the plantation housing popular during Hana's days as a sugar town. Recreational activities at the resort include pool and beach swimming, snorkeling, scuba diving, a three-hole practice golf course, croquet, horseback riding, hiking in the jungle, swimming near waterfalls, and exploring bamboo forests.

Executive chef, Amy Ferguson-Ota, honored as one of the "Twelve Great Women Chefs," is immersed in developing a cuisine that is a blend of Pacific Island, American, and Asian influences. Her specialties enhance the island's local ingredients. Chef Ferguson-Ota created the following dinner for two for *Menus and Music.*

Hotel Hana-Maui

THE MENU

Hotel Hana-Maui

Nori Fettuccine and Opihi with
Garlic-Chili Butter Sauce

Spicy Rack of Lamb with
Thai Red Curry Sauce

Mango Ice Cream Sandwich with
Macadamia Nut Cookies and
Tropical Fruit Compote

Nori Fettuccine and Opihi with
Garlic-Chili Butter Sauce

32 to 48 medium opihi,*
or 15 clams in their shells,
or ⅓ pound shelled cooked shrimp
3 cups unbleached all-purpose flour
1 teaspoon salt
1 small package (about ⅓ ounce) nori sheets**
1 ½ teaspoons Asian (toasted) sesame oil
1 tablespoon vegetable oil
1 tablespoon water
Garlic-Chili Butter Sauce (recipe follows)
Salt to taste

Shell the opihi. Place them in a small bowl, combine with two tablespoons of salt, and refrigerate overnight. Rinse off the salt with water before using. If clams are used, steam them in their shells until they open; shell and set aside.

In a blender or food processor, combine the flour, salt, and nori sheets until the nori is cut into small pieces and well blended with the flour. In a small bowl, blend the oils and water, and slowly add them to the flour mixture to form a moist dough. Let sit for 20 minutes. Roll out the dough and cut it into fettuccine using a pasta machine according to the manufacturer's instructions. In a large saucepan or stockpot, bring salted water to a rolling boil. Cook the nori fettuccine for 1 to 2 minutes and drain well. (Fresh pasta cooks very quickly, so be careful not to overcook.)

Hotel Hana-Maui

Serving. Toss the fettuccine with the opihi, clams, or shrimp and the warm garlic-chili butter sauce. Adjust the seasoning with salt if necessary. Serve in pasta bowls or on warm plates.

*Opihi are limpets gathered from the sea off the Hana coast.

**Nori, or seaweed, sheets are used in making sushi. They can be purchased at Asian grocery stores.

Garlic-Chili Butter Sauce

⅓ cup dry white wine
1 large garlic clove, minced
1 large shallot, minced
¼ teaspoon sambal olek *chili paste**
¼ cup heavy (whipping) cream
1 cup (2 sticks) unsalted butter, cut into small pieces
Salt to taste

In a small saucepan, simmer the wine, garlic, shallot, and chili paste until almost dry. Stir in the heavy cream and cook until the sauce thickens enough to coat the back of a spoon. Whip in the butter in small amounts over medium-low heat to form the sauce. Adjust the seasoning with salt.

Sambal olek chili paste is available in Asian markets.

Hotel Hana-Maui

Spicy Rack of Lamb with Thai Red Curry Sauce

1 tablespoon vegetable oil
One Frenched 2-pound rack of lamb
Salt and pepper to taste
Marinade (recipe follows)
Red Thai Curry Sauce (recipe follows)

Prepare the marinade and set it aside. In a large sauté pan or skillet, heat the oil to almost smoking and quickly brown the rack of lamb on all sides. Remove from the pan, season with salt and pepper, and set aside.

Place the lamb in the bowl with the marinade and marinate it for 2 to 4 hours in the refrigerator.

Preheat the oven to 400° F. Place the marinated lamb in a roasting pan and bake in the preheated oven for 20 minutes, or until the thickest part of the roast reaches an internal temperature of 125° F for rosy rare, 140° F for medium rare, or 180° F for well done. Remove the roasting pan from the oven and let the lamb sit for 10 minutes before carving.

Serving. Cut the lamb into 2-rib portions. Spoon the Thai red curry sauce onto 2 plates and place the double-cut lamb chops on top.

Hotel Hana-Maui

Marinade

4 tablespoons hoisin sauce
3 tablespoons honey
2 tablespoons dark soy sauce
2 tablespoons dry sherry
1 tablespoon Asian (toasted) sesame oil
1 tablespoon curry powder
1 teaspoon sambal olek *chili paste*
4 garlic cloves, minced
1 tablespoon minced orange zest (page 86)
1 tablespoon Chinese salted black beans, chopped
1 tablespoon Thai red curry paste
¼ cup sesame seeds

In a glass or ceramic mixing bowl large enough to hold the lamb, stir together all the marinade ingredients.

Thai Red Curry Sauce

1 ½ cups Lamb Stock (page 224) or reduced canned chicken broth
1 tablespoon Thai red curry paste
1 tablespoon butter
1 teaspoon chopped fresh cilantro

In a saucepan over high heat, reduce the lamb stock or beef broth by half to make a demi-glace. Stir in the red Thai curry paste, then whip in the butter in order to thicken the sauce. Add the cilantro just before serving the sauce.

*The hoisin sauce, dark soy sauce, *sambal olek* chili paste, Chinese salted black beans, and Thai red curry paste are all available in Asian markets.

Hotel Hana-Maui

Mango Ice Cream Sandwich with
Macadamia Nut Cookies and Tropical Fruit Compote

Mango Purée

2 ripe mangoes*

Peel and seed the mangoes; cut them into cubes and purée in blender or food processor.

*Chef Amy Ferguson-Ota uses Hayden mangoes from Hawaii, and they are the preferred ingredient.

Mango Ice Cream

6 tablespoons mango purée, above
½ cup half and half
½ cup sugar
3 egg yolks
1 ¼ cups heavy (whipping) cream

In a small saucepan, stir together the half and half and sugar over medium-low heat until the sugar dissolves. Add the egg yolks one at a time to the half and half mixture to form a custard, stirring constantly so the eggs don't curdle. Remove from heat and let cool to room temperature. Stir in the heavy cream and mango purée. Freeze in an ice cream machine according to the directions supplied by the manufacturer.

Hotel Hana-Maui

Macadamia Nut Cookies

*½ cup (1 stick) plus 3 tablespoons unsalted butter
at room temperature*
½ cup sugar
1 egg
¼ teaspoon vanilla extract
1 cup unbleached all-purpose flour
3 tablespoons unsalted macadamia nuts, chopped

Preheat the oven to 350° F. Cream together the butter and sugar until light and fluffy. Add the egg and vanilla. Gradually fold in the flour and nuts, blending just until smooth. Place large spoonfuls of the dough onto a lightly greased baking sheet, and bake for 10 to 12 minutes. Let cool.

Tropical Fruit Compote

1 ripe mango, peeled and seeded
2 kiwi fruit, peeled
½ cup fresh or unsweetened canned pineapple chunks
½ cup ripe ohelo berries* or raspberries
Sugar or honey to taste

Cut the mango, kiwi, and pineapple into consistent-sized pieces. In a mixing bowl, combine with the ohelo berries or raspberries and sweeten with sugar or honey, if desired. (Often no sweetener is needed because of the fruits' natural sweetness.)

*Ohelo berries are red currant-like berries that grow in the high altitudes of the islands of Maui and Hawaii.

Hotel Hana-Maui

Assembling the Ice Cream Sandwich

The prepared ice cream
The prepared cookies
The prepared compote

Place a soft scoop of mango ice cream between 2 macadamia nut cookies. Repeat to make a second sandwich. Slightly flatten the ice cream, wrap the sandwiches in plastic wrap, and freeze until the ice cream hardens.

Serving. Spoon some of the remaining mango purée onto 2 plates. Cut the ice cream sandwiches in half and place on the plates on top of the purée. Spoon the tropical fruit compote in a mound beside the ice cream sandwiches.

THE INN AT LITTLE WASHINGTON

Washington, Virginia

The Inn at Little Washington is located in the one-stop-sign hamlet of Washington which was surveyed by the young George Washington in 1749. The town is only an hour and a half's drive from "Big" Washington, D.C. Owners Reinhardt Lynch and Patrick O'Connell's dedication to excellence has transformed their turn-of-the-century building, which had served as a garage and country store, into a magnificent restaurant and inn. The Inn at Little Washington became America's first inn ever to receive the Mobil Travel Guide's Five-Star Award and the first inn to receive the American Automobile Association's Five-Diamond Award for both its restaurant and accommodations. The Inn is also a member of the prestigious Relais & Chateaux.

Lynch and O'Connell opened their restaurant in 1978 and immediately had clientele arriving from the nation's capital; more than three thousand people have requested seating for their Saturday-night dinner for 120. In 1984 eight guest rooms were added above the restaurant; two duplex suites were added later. All rooms and suites at the Inn are lavishly furnished with English antiques and lush fabrics in the comfortable manner of an English country house. Guests at the Inn can enjoy outdoor beauty in the nearby Blue Ridge Mountains, Shenandoah National Park, and Luray Caverns.

The Inn's restaurant is the heart of the Inn. It surrounds a charming interior courtyard with a gazebo and is utterly romantic. Chef Patrick O'Connell is a culinary artist whose imaginative and personal adaptation of classic French cuisine with regional specialties has won raves from food critics and earned the restaurant a Relais Gourmand rating. Chef O'Connell created the following holiday dinner for two and presented it to *Menus and Music*.

The Inn at Little Washington

THE MENU

The Inn at Little Washington

A Holiday Menu

*Baby Boudins Blancs with
Sauerkraut Braised in Riesling*

Champagne Sorbet

*Medallions of Veal, Lamb, and Venison with
Wild Mushrooms, Shallots, and Lingonberry Salsa*

Warm Apple-Walnut Rose

Baby Boudins Blancs with
Sauerkraut Braised in Riesling

Sausage

½ pound veal

¼ pound boneless chicken breast, skinned

4 ounces pork fatback, trimmed of rind, or rinsed salt pork

½ cup half and half

¼ large onion

1 egg white

¾ cup French bread crumbs (remove crusts before grinding)

2 tablespoons green peppercorns

1 tablespoon freshly ground black pepper

1 tablespoon freshly grated nutmeg

Pinch of ground cinnamon

Pinch of ground cloves

Pinch of ground allspice

½ tablespoon salt

½ tablespoon minced garlic

2 small hog casings from your butcher,
soaked in cold water for 1 hour

Grind the veal, chicken, and fatback, and set aside. (The chicken can be ground by processing it in a food processor while it is half frozen.)

In a small saucepan, place the half and half and onion, and bring to a boil. Remove from heat and let stand for 10 minutes before removing the onion. Set the liquid aside to cool.

In a medium bowl, thoroughly combine the ground meat, cooled half and half, egg white, bread crumbs, green peppercorns, spices, salt, and garlic. Form a small portion of the mixture into a patty and fry it to test the seasoning. Adjust seasoning to taste.

The Inn at Little Washington

With a sausage stuffer, press the meat mixture into the hog casings, and tie off with cotton string to make small sausages.

Note: The sausages can be prepared in advance, and will keep 2 days or so under refrigeration.

Sauerkraut Braised in Riesling

1 ½ pounds fresh sauerkraut,
drained and soaked overnight in a large bowl of cold water
3 bacon slices, diced
¼ onion, diced
1 apple, peeled, cored, and diced
1 tablespoon juniper berries, minced
2 bay leaves
½ bottle Riesling*
Sugar, salt, and pepper to taste

Preheat the oven to 325° F. Drain and rinse the sauerkraut. Press it dry and pick apart to separate the strands. Set aside.

In a sauté pan or skillet, sauté the bacon until brown. Add the onion, apple, and juniper berries, and sauté until tender. Stir in the sauerkraut, bay leaves, and Riesling, and bring to a simmer. Place a lid on the pan and simmer for about 10 minutes. Remove from the flame and place in the preheated oven, uncovered; cook until most of the liquid evaporates. Remove from the oven, remove and discard the bay leaves, and season the sauerkraut with the sugar, salt, and pepper.

Note: The sauerkraut may be cooked ahead, left uncovered until cool, then covered and refrigerated.

*Chef Patrick O'Connor uses Virginia Riesling, and this is the preferred ingredient if you can find it.

The Inn at Little Washington

Poaching the Sausages

4 cups milk

4 cups water

1 carrot, peeled and chopped

1 celery stalk, chopped

1 onion, chopped

In a large saucepan place the milk, water, carrot, celery, and onion and bring to a boil. Add the sausages, remove the pan from heat, and let stand, covered, for 10 minutes. Remove the sausages with a slotted spoon and allow them to cool. Film a sauté pan or skillet with oil; fry the sausages slowly, turning frequently, until golden brown and heated through.

Serving. Divide the sausages and sauerkraut between 2 plates.

The Inn at Little Washington

Champagne Sorbet

1 cup water
1 ¼ cups sugar
½ bottle champagne
Juice of 1 lemon
Pinch of grated lemon zest (page 86)

In a medium saucepan, combine the water and sugar and cook over medium heat, stirring until the sugar completely dissolves. Continue cooking at a simmer for 5 minutes; remove from the heat and let cool. Stir in the champagne, lemon juice, and lemon zest. Pour this mixture into an ice cream maker and freeze according to the manufacturer's instructions. Serve in chilled champagne or martini glasses.

Variation: In a large bowl, beat 2 egg whites until soft peaks form; beat in 2 tablespoons sugar until firm peaks form. When the sorbet is almost frozen, fold in the meringue and continue freezing.

The Inn at Little Washington

Medallions of Veal, Lamb, and Venison with
Wild Mushrooms, Shallots, and Lingonberry Salsa

Mushrooms

2 ounces shiitake mushrooms

2 ounces trumpet mushrooms

2 ounces chanterelle mushrooms

1 tablespoon flour

Salt and freshly ground pepper to taste

2 tablespoons butter

Clean and stem the mushrooms, reserving stems. Cut the mushroom caps into medium pieces. Lighlty flour the mushrooms and season with salt and pepper. In a sauté pan or skillet, melt the butter and sauté the mushrooms until crisp and lightly browned. Just before serving, warm the mushrooms over low heat.

Mushroom Sauce

1 tablespoon vegetable oil

1 tablespoon chopped shallots

½ bunch parsley, stemmed and minced

3 garlic cloves, minced

½ bunch chopped fresh rosemary

Reserved mushroom stems (about ½ cup), chopped

½ tablespoon minced fresh tarragon

1 bay leaf

1 cup burgundy

1 quart Veal Stock (page 226) or reduced canned chicken broth

½ large tomato, chopped

Salt and pepper to taste

In a medium saucepan, heat the oil over medium-high heat and cook the shallots, parsley, garlic, rosemary, chopped mushroom stems, tarragon, and bay leaf until

The Inn at Little Washington

the shallots are translucent. Increase the heat to high, add the burgundy, and reduce the liquid by half. Add the veal stock or chicken broth and reduce by half. Add the tomato and adjust the seasoning. Strain through a sieve. Just before serving, warm the sauce over low heat.

Lingonberry Salsa

⅓ cup whole shallots, peeled
1 dried ancho chili, stemmed and seeded
2 tablespoons diced jalapeño
½ cup preserved lingonberries
1 teaspoon fresh lime juice

In a blender or food processor, place the shallots and ancho chili and chop coarsely at low speed. Transfer to a mixing bowl and combine with the jalapeño, lingonberries, and lime juice.

Note: The salsa can be prepared in advance. Covered and refrigerated, it will keep for 3 to 4 days.

The Inn at Little Washington

To Cook and Garnish the Medallions

1 tablespoon vegetable oil
Two 3-ounce veal medallions*
Two 3-ounce lamb medallions
Two 3-ounce venison or beef medallions**
¼ cup dry white wine
Salt and freshly ground pepper to taste
Fresh or preserved lingonberries for garnish
1 ½ shallots, minced, for garnish

Preheat the oven to 350° F. Season the medallions with salt and pepper. Film a hot sauté pan or skillet with the oil, place the medallions in the pan, and quickly sear both sides. Deglaze the pan with the white wine, season with salt and pepper, and finish cooking the meat in the oven for 3 to 5 minutes.

Serving. Arrange the veal, lamb, and venison medallions on each of 2 plates in a circle. Mound the sautéed mushrooms in the center of the meats. Pool the warm mushroom sauce around the meats and sprinkle the lingonberries and chopped shallots over the meats. Garnish with lingonberry salsa.

 *A medallion is a round fillet cut from the loin or tenderloin. A butcher dealing in high-quality meats will prepare them for you.

**Venison is available at some butcher shops and specialty food shops. It can be ordered directly from D'Artagnan by calling (800) DARTAGNAN or, in New Jersey, (201) 792-0748.

The Inn at Little Washington

Warm Apple Walnut Rose

Walnut Cream

⅔ cup sugar
½ cup (1 stick) unsalted butter, softened
2 tablespoons flour
1 ½ cups chopped walnuts
1 egg
1 teaspoon vanilla extract
1 ½ tablespoons applejack

In a medium bowl, beat together the sugar and butter until light and fluffy. Blend in the flour, walnuts, egg, vanilla, and applejack. Chill in the refrigerator.

Note: The walnut cream can be prepared ahead and kept in the refrigerator for several days.

Apple Filling

2 apples, peeled, halved, and cored
1 teaspoon rum, or to taste
½ teaspoon fresh lemon juice, or to taste
1 tablespoon sugar, or to taste
2 whole cloves
½ cinnamon stick, halved
Fresh lemon juice to taste
Vanilla extract to taste

Preheat the oven to 375° F. In a jelly-roll pan, lay the apples close together, flat side down, and sprinkle with the rum, lemon juice, sugar, cloves, and cinnamon stick. Cover with aluminum foil and bake in the oven for 20 minutes, or until the

The Inn at Little Washington

apples are just tender. Remove from the oven and cool. Remove the cinnamon sticks and cloves. Cut the apples into ½-inch chunks and mix with the walnut cream. Season to taste with lemon juice and vanilla.

Assembling and Garnishing the Rose

2 sheets filo dough (about 16 by 14 inches each), thawed
Prepared filling
Carmel sauce, such as the one on page 192
2 tablespoons sour cream, sweetened with ½ teaspoon sugar

Preheat the oven to 375° F. If you have a convection or a second oven, also preheat it, to 425° F. Wrap the walnut cream and apple filling in 2 large pieces of filo and fold the filo in half. Fold the filo again into quarters and arrange the sheets in the center of the pastry in a rose design. Bake in the preheated 375° F oven for 3 minutes; then transfer to the oven preheated to 425° F. Bake until golden, about 10 minutes. If you do not have a second oven, raise the oven temperature to 425° F for 10 minutes, place the the rose in the oven, and bake until golden.

Serving. Spoon some of the warm caramel sauce onto 2 plates. Swirl the sweetened sour cream into the caramel. Place a warm apple walnut rose on top of the sauce and serve immediately.

The Inn at Little Washington

THE INN AT MANITOU

LAKESIDE SPA & TENNIS RESORT

McKellar, Ontario

The Inn at Manitou is a small, casually elegant resort located on the shores of Lake Manitouwabing, just north of Toronto. The resort is the creation of Ben and Sheila Wise. They have combined a world-class tennis club and a new health and beauty spa with luxurious lodgings, refined service, and gourmet cuisine amid beautiful, unspoiled surroundings. The Inn at Manitou is an award-winning member of Relais & Chateaux.

The Inn's gracious accommodations are clustered near the tennis courts and on a knoll above the lake. Guests enjoy tennis on the resort's thirteen courts, and fourteen competent pros cater to the guests' volleys and serves. The tennis program of clinics and instruction is tailored to the needs of players at every level. Guests also can enjoy treatments at the Inn's new fitness, health, and beauty spa facility. Other recreational pursuits include heated-pool swimming, horseback riding, windsurfing, boating, mountain biking, aerobics classes, and massage services.

The Inn at Manitou has been a luxury resort from its beginning, and great food has played an important part from the first day. The Inn's remarkable French cuisine has a world-wide reputation and now, for fitness-conscious guests, spa food is also offered. The dining room is candlelit, and there is a nightly performance of piano music. Chef Jean Pierre Challet created the following dinner for two for *Menus and Music.*

The Inn at Manitou

THE MENU

The Inn at Manitou

*Beet Consommé with
Vegetables, Salmon, and Scallops*

Goose Liver with Red Pepper and Lavender Honey

Spiced Cornish Hen Stuffed with Shrimp

Raspberries Jubilee with Kahlúa

Beet Consommé with
Vegetables, Salmon, and Scallops

Beet Consommé with Vegetables

2 small beets
2 egg whites
Minced fresh cilantro, thyme, chives, and green onion to taste
Freshly ground black pepper to taste
2 cups Fish Stock (page 222) or clam juice
2 asparagus spears
2 baby carrots, peeled
1 small leek
2 tiny new potatoes

Cut off the tops of the beets, then peel and grate them. In a small bowl, combine the grated beets, egg whites, cilantro, thyme, chives, green onion, and pepper. In a saucepan, heat the fish stock or clam juice just until it simmers, add the egg mixture, then heat until just boiling, gently stirring all the while. Reduce to a simmer and cook for 30 minutes. Remove the pan from the heat and carefully strain the consommé through a sieve.

Return the consommé to the pan, bring to a simmer, and poach the asparagus, carrots, leek, and potatoes until just tender. Remove the vegetables with a slotted spoon just before serving.

Cooking and Garnishing the Salmon and Scallops

2 sea scallops
One 4-ounce salmon steak
1 tablespoon clarified butter (page 220) or vegetable oil
Minced fresh cilantro, thyme, chives, and green onion for garnish

Wash and dry the salmon and scallops. Place a sauté pan or skillet over medium-high heat and film the bottom of the pan with clarified butter or vegetable oil.

The Inn at Manitou

When the butter or oil is hot but not burning, add the salmon steak. Sauté for about 5 minutes on each side. Remove from the pan. Sauté the scallops over high heat, tossing, until the scallops feel lightly springy to the touch, a total of 2 to 3 minutes.

Serving. Immediately divide the salmon and scallops between 2 shallow soup bowls. Divide the poached vegetables between the bowls, pour the hot consommé over, and sprinkle with fresh cilantro, thyme, chives, and green onion.

The Inn at Manitou

Goose Liver with Red Pepper and Lavender Honey Sauce

½ red bell pepper, cored and seeded
1 poached artichoke bottom (page 159)
5 ounces fresh goose or duck liver*
1 tablespoon clarified butter (page 220)
Red Pepper and Lavender Honey Sauce (recipe follows)
1 green onion, chopped, for garnish

Cut the halved red pepper and artichoke heart bottom into thick matchsticks and set aside.

Slice the goose liver into ¼-inch thick slices with a sharp knife that has been dipped in boiling water for each slice. Cover the slices and chill for at least 20 minutes, or until cooking time. (The liver is chilled so that a minimum of fat will exude during cooking.) Film the bottom of a sauté pan or skillet with the clarified butter and heat to very hot but not burning. Rapidly sauté the foie gras slices one at a time less than a minute on each side, or until just brown around the edges.

Serving. Spoon the red pepper and honey sauce in the middle of each of 2 plates. Place the goose liver slices on top of the sauce, and top with the sticks of artichoke bottom and red pepper. Sprinkle with chopped green onion.

*If your specialty market or the poultry section of the yellow pages cannot help you find goose liver, you could try D'Artagnan in Jersey City, New Jersey. Telephone (800) 327-8246 (mail orders are available UPS Next Day Air).

The Inn at Manitou

Red Pepper and Lavender Honey Sauce

1 red pepper, cored and seeded
1 shallot
1 tablespoon lavender or other wildflower honey
1 ½ teaspoons balsamic vinegar
½ cup Chicken Stock (page 220) or canned chicken broth
Salt and pepper to taste

Coarsely chop the red pepper and shallot. In a sauté pan or skillet, sauté the pepper and shallot with the honey over medium heat until the pepper is soft. Stir in the vinegar, add the chicken stock or broth, and boil to reduce the liquid by half. Season with salt and pepper. Transfer to a blender or food processor and purée until smooth. Strain through a sieve and set aside.

The Inn at Manitou

Spiced Cornish Hen Stuffed with Shrimp

1 Cornish game hen
4 shrimp
1 tablespoon honey
½ teaspoon ground cumin
½ teaspoon dried oregano
¼ teaspoon ground coriander
Pinch of saffron
1 cup Chicken Stock (page 220) or canned chicken broth
Mashed Potatoes (recipe follows)

Preheat the oven to 350° F. Stuff the hen with the shrimp and truss the hen. In a large saucepan, bring the chicken stock or broth to a simmer and poach the Cornish game hen for 1 minute; remove the hen and reserve the stock. In a small bowl, combine the honey, cumin, oregano, coriander, and saffron. Brush the hen with the honey mixture, then pour the rest of the honey mixture on the bottom of a baking pan. Place the hen on top and bake in the preheated oven for about 45 minutes, or until the hen reaches 180° F on a meat thermometer inserted at the inner thigh.

Serving. Place a few tablespoons of mashed potatoes in the middle of each plate. Cut the hen in half, and arrange the hen and shrimp on top of the potatoes. Deglaze the baking pan with the reserved chicken stock or broth, and reduce the sauce by half. Spoon the sauce around the potatoes.

Mashed Potatoes

2 large russet potatoes
2 tablespoons hot milk
1 or more tablespoons softened butter
Salt and freshly ground white pepper to taste

Wash and peel the potatoes and cut into quarters. Place in a saucepan with lightly salted water to cover. Bring to a boil, cover, and boil 10 to 15 minutes or longer, or until the potatoes are tender when pierced with a knife. Drain the water out of the pan and mash the potatoes with the milk and butter. Season with salt and pepper to taste and serve immediately.

Raspberries Jubilee with Kahlúa

2 ounces fresh (page 191) or defrosted frozen puff pastry
1 egg white, beaten
1 tablespoon sifted powdered sugar
2 tablespoons Grand Marnier
2 tablespoons Kahlúa
1 tablespoon raspberry liqueur (framboise)
1 basket raspberries, or one 10-ounce package
unsweetened frozen raspberries, defrosted
2 scoops vanilla ice cream

Cut the puff pastry into two 4-inch rounds. Brush the top of each with beaten egg white and sprinkle with powdered sugar. Put in the freezer and chill for about 30 minutes. Meanwhile, preheat the oven to 425° F for at least 20 minutes. Place the pastry on a baking sheet covered with parchment or greased with butter. Bake in the preheated oven for 4 minutes. Reduce the oven temperature to 375° F and continue baking until the pastry turns golden brown, about 5 to 10 minutes. Let cool.

In a small saucepan, cook the Grand Marnier, Kahlúa, and raspberry liqueur over medium heat to reduce the liquid by half. Remove from the heat and fold the raspberries into the syrup to just heat through.

The Inn at Manitou

Serving. Slice off the top half of each cooled pastry round. Spoon the ice cream inside, and pour the warm raspberries and syrup over the ice cream. Cover with pastry tops and serve immediately.

The Inn at Manitou

THE INN AT SAWMILL FARM

West Dover, Vermont

Not far from major East Coast cities, guests at The Inn at Sawmill Farm enjoy quiet pleasures near a Vermont village. In 1968, Rodney Williams, architect, and Ione Williams, interior designer, purchased a Vermont farmhouse built in 1897 as a vacation home and began a loving restoration. The vacation home has evolved into an intimate country inn of exceptional quality and charm. There are now twenty-one rooms and suites set on more than twenty acres. The Inn's large common room is filled with English chintzes and antiques, and the glow of a walk-in fireplace beckons with the warmth of a private home. The bedchambers upstairs in the main building exude comfort and serenity. The Williams have added small cottages with fireplaces that are grouped around the property's old barn, and guest rooms in homes that were originally built for their children. In addition to its Relais & Chateaux membership, The Inn at Sawmill Farm has been awarded a Four-Star Award by the Mobil Travel Guide.

In winter, the New England landscape offers exceptional downhill and cross-country skiing, and snowshoe hikes into wooded areas. In warmer weather, the Inn's own pool and tennis court, and Mount Snow's championship golf course are popular. Guests also can enjoy fishing in the Inn's trout ponds, antiquing, country auctions, and the world-famous Marlboro Music Festival.

Rodney and Ione's son, Brill Williams, is the Inn's chef and a respected oenophile. He has selected over thirty thousand bottles of wine for the inn's three cellars; a collection that is acclaimed as one of the top one hundred in the United States. The Inn at Sawmill Farm's restaurant serves outstanding American-Continental cuisine. Chef Brill Williams created the following dinner for two for *Menus and Music*.

The Inn at Sawmill Farm

THE MENU

The Inn at Sawmill Farm

Sautéed Scallops in Curry Sauce

Poached Salmon and Sole with Tarragon Sauce

Brandy Apple Cake with Grand Marnier Sauce

Sautéed Scallops in Curry Sauce

1 small honeydew melon
1 small cantaloupe
10 sea scallops, cut into thirds or fourths
1 tablespoon butter
Curry Sauce (recipe follows)

Cut the honeydew and the cantaloupe in half. Seed and scoop the melons into small melon balls; set aside.

Carefully wash the scallops in cold water and pat them dry with paper towels. In a sauté pan or skillet, melt the butter and sauté the scallops over high heat, tossing to lightly brown on all sides, a total of 2 to 3 minutes. Remove from the heat and drain the butter from the pan. Add the melon balls and warm curry sauce. Stir to combine. To serve, divide the scallops and curry sauce between 2 plates.

Curry Sauce

¼ cup dry white vermouth
½ cup Chicken Stock (page 220) or canned chicken broth
¼ cup Fish Stock (page 222) or clam juice
½ cup pineapple juice
½ apple, peeled, cored, and chopped
¼ banana, peeled and chopped
1 tablespoon curry powder
2 tablespoons chopped shallots
1 ½ tablespoons butter
2 tablespoons flour
½ cup heavy (whipping) cream
Salt and pepper to taste

The Inn at Sawmill Farm

In a medium saucepan, mix together the vermouth, chicken stock or broth, fish stock or clam juice, pineapple juice, apple, banana, curry powder, and shallots. Cook over high heat and reduce by half.

In a heavy saucepan, melt the butter and add the flour; stir over low heat for 2 minutes. Whisking constantly, gradually add the curry mixture to the butter and flour to make a thick sauce. Fold in the cream and remove from the heat. Strain the sauce through a sieve and season with salt and pepper.

The Inn at Sawmill Farm

Poached Salmon and Sole with Tarragon Sauce

Court Bouillon

2 cups water

4 parsley sprigs

2 celery leaves

1 bay leaf

¼ teaspoon cracked peppercorns

A few fennel seeds or aniseeds

½ small onion, cut into quarters

½ cup dry white wine, or ⅛ cup fresh lemon juice

In a large saucepan, bring all the ingredients to a boil and simmer for 20 minutes. Remove from the heat and strain through a sieve; set aside.

Fish

One 6-by-2-inch salmon fillet, split in half lengthwise

One 6-ounce fillet of sole, split in half lengthwise

2 cups court bouillon, above

Preheat the oven to 475° F. Roll the salmon fillet strips from head to tail and repeat with the strips of sole fillets. Place the salmon and sole rolls in an ovenproof sauté pan or skillet and cover them with court bouillon. Bake in the preheated oven for 6 to 7 minutes. Carefully remove the fish rolls from the court bouillon with a slotted spoon. Reserve this liquid for the tarragon sauce.

The Inn at Sawmill Farm

Tarragon Sauce

½ cup reserved fish poaching liquid or clam juice
½ cup dry white wine
2 shallots, chopped
1 plum tomato, chopped
7 ½ tablespoons chopped fresh tarragon
½ tablespoon tarragon vinegar (page 41)
2 thyme sprigs
½ cup heavy (whipping) cream
Salt and pepper to taste

In a large saucepan, add the fish poaching liquid or clam juice, white wine, shallots, tomato, tarragon, vinegar, and thyme. Cook over high heat to reduce the liquid by one fourth. Stir in the heavy cream and remove from heat. Strain the sauce through a fine sieve and season with salt and pepper; return to very low heat to keep warm.

Serving. Arrange the salmon and sole rolls on 2 plates. Spoon the warm tarragon sauce over.

The Inn at Sawmill Farm

Brandy Apple Cake with Grand Marnier Sauce

½ cup raisins
2 cups chopped peeled apples
⅓ cup brandy
1 cup sugar
¼ cup vegetable oil
1 egg
½ cup chopped walnuts
1 cup sifted unbleached all-purpose flour
1 teaspoon ground cinnamon
½ teaspoon ground nutmeg
¼ teaspoon ground cloves
1 teaspoon baking soda
½ teaspoon salt
Grand Marnier Sauce (recipe follows)

Preheat the oven to 325° F. In a small bowl, pour boiling water over the raisins to cover them and soak for 5 minutes to soften; drain. Place the chopped apples in a medium bowl, pour the brandy over, and stir to coat them with brandy. In a large bowl, whisk together the sugar, oil, and egg. In a medium bowl, sift together the flour, cinnamon, nutmeg, cloves, baking soda, and salt; stir in the walnuts and raisins. Combine the apples with the sugar mixture, then add the flour mixture, mixing until well blended.

Fold the batter into a buttered 8-inch-square baking pan. Bake in the preheated oven for 50 to 60 minutes, or until a cake tester comes out clean. Serve warm or cold with Grand Marnier sauce.

The Inn at Sawmill Farm

Grand Marnier Sauce

1 egg
¼ cup sugar
¾ tablespoon cornstarch
1 cup half and half
¼ teaspoon vanilla extract
½ cup heavy (whipping) cream
Grand Marnier (1 or 2 tablespoons) or to taste

In the top of a double boiler, mix together the egg, sugar, and cornstarch over boiling water. Add the half and half and cook without allowing to boil until the mixture has thickened enough to coat the back of a spoon. Remove the pan from the heat and add the vanilla. Cover the sauce with buttered waxed paper and let cool completely.

Just before serving, beat the heavy cream until soft peaks form. Fold the whipped cream into the cooled sauce, add the Grand Marnier to taste, and gently blend.

The Inn at Sawmill Farm

LA COLOMBE D'OR

Houston, Texas

     La Colombe d'Or offers European charm and intimate luxury in the vibrant city of Houston, Texas. Built in 1923 as a private residence for Walter Fondren, the founder of Exxon, it is now distinguished by a Texas Historical Marker. The graceful twenty-one-room mansion has been transformed into a small hotel and superb restaurant by Stephen Zimmerman, who purchased the property in 1979. During his travels abroad, Mr. Zimmerman deepened his interest in fine food, wine, and art, and his enjoyment of the numerous three-star auberges in the South of France prompted him to model his own property after these delightful inns.

     La Colombe d'Or has six spacious suites, each with its own dining room and decorated with a comfortable mixture of contemporary and Victorian furnishings and striking modern art. Most guests prefer to dine downstairs in the romantic surroundings of La Colombe d'Or's innovative French restaurant, which is distinguished as one of only four Relais Gourmands in the United States. Guests may enjoy the hotel's four luxurious dining rooms, the intimate walnut-paneled bar, the cozy firelit library, and a sculpture garden. Executive chef Fabrice Beaudoin created the following dinner for two for *Menus and Music*.

THE MENU

La Colombe d'Or

Marinated Shrimp in a Coulis of Tomato, Orange, and Ginger

*Smoked Squab Salad with a Fricassee of
Golden Chanterelle Mushrooms*

*Grilled Beef Tournedos and Consommé
with Baby Vegetables*

Fresh Berries with Cassis Sherbet and Champagne

Marinated Shrimp in a Coulis of Tomato, Orange, and Ginger

16 shelled fava (broad) beans, or 1 cup asparagus tips
3 tablespoons olive oil
12 jumbo shrimp (16 to 20 per pound), peeled and deveined
Tomato, Orange, and Ginger Coulis (recipe follows)
2 mint sprigs for garnish

In a saucepan, blanch the fava beans in boiling salted water to cover for 15 seconds. Remove with a slotted spoon and peel; set aside.

In a sauté pan or skillet, heat the olive oil over medium-high heat and sauté the shrimp just until they turn evenly pink. Add the cooked shrimp to the coulis and let sit for 1 hour at room temperature to let the flavors combine.

Serving. Divide the coulis and shrimp between 2 shallow soup bowls. Garnish with the fava beans or asparagus tips and mint sprigs.

Tomato, Orange, and Ginger Coulis

3 large tomatoes
4 blood oranges or 2 navel oranges, peeled and divided into segments
½ teaspoon grated fresh ginger
1 cup freshly squeezed orange juice
3 tablespoons honey
1 unpeeled garlic clove
Salt and cayenne pepper to taste
2 each oregano, parsley, and thyme sprigs and
one 1-inch piece lemon grass wrapped in cheesecloth and tied

Drop the tomatoes into a pot of boiling water for 1 to 2 minutes, remove with a slotted spoon, and place them into a bowl of ice water. Cut out a small cone around the stem ends and slip off the skins. To seed the tomatoes, cut in half and gently squeeze over a bowl, or a sieve if you want to save the juice. The seeds will drop out. Pick out any remaining seeds with your finger or a spoon. Chop the tomatoes.

In a heavy sauté pan or skillet, combine all the coulis ingredients. Cook over a medium high heat until the liquid reduces by three fourths. Remove from the heat and remove the garlic clove and herb bag.

Smoked Squab Salad with a Fricassee of
Golden Chanterelle Mushrooms

Marinated and Smoked Squab

Two 1-pound squabs, or 2 Cornish game hens
1 star anise
1 cinnamon stick
10 black peppercorns
5 whole cloves
1 teaspoon ground coriander
1 teaspoon chopped fresh thyme
1 teaspoon kosher salt
1 teaspoon brown sugar
2 tablespoons butter
2 tablespoons red wine vinegar

First cut out the backbones of the squabs or hens so they can be spread flat. Heavily lean on the squabs or hens to crack the breast and rib bones. Be careful not to break through the breast meat and skin. Bone the breasts, but leave the leg bones in and the skin on.

Using a mortar and pestle or spice grinder, grind all the spices and herbs. In a stock pot or saucepan, place the squab bones, ground spices and herbs, salt, brown sugar, and water to cover. Bring to a boil, reduce the heat to a simmer, and cook uncovered for about 2 hours, skimming the surface occasionally to remove any foam. Add water as needed so that ingredients are always covered. Place the squab or hens in the stock, cover, and marinate 12 to 24 hours in the refrigerator.

Remove the birds from the stock. Strain the stock through a sieve, and refrigerate in a covered container until needed.

Smoke the squab in a wood-burning smoker for 10 minutes, following the manufacturer's instructions. In a large sauté pan or skillet, melt the butter and

La Colombe d'Or

sauté the squab until medium rare, about 10 to 20 minutes. Remove the birds from the pan and pour in the red wine vinegar; boil and stir to deglaze the pan. Pour the reserved stock into the pan and boil to reduce to a syrup. Glaze the squab with the reduced stock.

Salad Dressing

3 tablespoons olive oil
2 tablespoons walnut oil
1 to 2 tablespoons red wine vinegar
1 finely minced shallot
Salt and pepper to taste

In a mixing bowl, whisk together the olive oil, walnut oil, vinegar, shallot, salt, and pepper until thoroughly combined.

Fricassee of Golden Chanterelle Mushrooms

6 golden chanterelle mushrooms
1 tablespoon butter
½ garlic clove
½ shallot, minced
Salt and pepper to taste
1 teaspoon chopped fresh chives

Trim, wash, and dry the mushrooms; cut them into slices. In a sauté pan or skillet, melt the butter and sauté the garlic and shallot over medium-low heat until the shallot is translucent. Add the chanterelles and sauté for about 2 minutes. Remove from the heat, season lightly with salt and pepper, and sprinkle with the chives.

La Colombe d'Or

Salad Greens

1 Belgium endive

2 handfuls mixed salad greens such as mesclun, arugula, Italian parsley, mint leaves, tarragon leaves, watercress, and celery leaves

Just before serving, toss the salad greens with the dressing until all the leaves are lightly and uniformly coated.

Serving. Divide the greens between 2 salad plates, place the squab or hens on top of the salad, and pour the sauce over. Garnish with the chanterelle fricassee.

Grilled Beef Tournedos and
Consommé with Baby Vegetables

Consommé

2 yellow onions

1 tablespoon olive oil

3 carrots, peeled

2 turnips

3 leeks, green part only

3 celery stalks

½ beef shank

2 chicken carcasses, bones and trimmings

5 garlic cloves, unpeeled

*3 parsley sprigs, 2 thyme sprigs, and
1 bay leaf wrapped in cheesecloth and tied*

*3 black peppercorns, 2 whole cloves, and
5 coriander seeds wrapped in cheesecloth and tied*

Light a charcoal fire in an open grill. Peel the yellow onions and cut them in half. Brush the cut side of the onions with olive oil, and place them, oiled side down, on the grill over very hot coals. Cook the onions until brown, then remove them from the grill using a spatula. Coarsely chop the carrots, turnips, leeks, and celery.

In a large stockpot, place the beef shank and chicken parts with cold water to cover. Bring to a boil and skim off the foam. Add the grilled onion, chopped vegetables, garlic, and the herbs and spices. Reduce the heat to a simmer and cook for 4 hours, adding water as needed so that the ingredients are always covered. Skim off the fat and strain the consommé through a fine sieve.

Note: This consommé can be made ahead of time. Let cool, refrigerate, and then reheat. It makes a delicious bouillon for other meals.

Baby Vegetables

2 baby red potatoes
1 tablespoon olive oil
4 baby carrots
4 baby white turnips, peeled
2 baby yellow squash
8 green beans, trimmed
1 small fennel bulb
8 trimmed green onions
4 ears baby corn
8 asparagus, trimmed
2 baby leeks, timmed
8 snow peas

In a small pot, put the potatoes in lightly salted water to cover, bring to a boil, and cook for 10 minutes, or until tender when pierced with a knife. Remove from the water, and cut each potato into 4 quarters. Allow the potatoes to cool slightly, coat them with the olive oil, and thread them on metal skewers. Place the skewers over very hot coals and cook, turning once, until browned. Remove from the grill and set aside.

Using a paring knife, slice the carrots, turnips, squash, and green beans into similar-size pieces. Trim the fennel stalks down to the bulb, trim the bottom, then quarter and slice crosswise. Cook all the vegetables in the consommé until they are tender.

La Colombe d'Or

Beef Tournedos

2 6-ounce beef tournedos
Salt and pepper to taste
2 split beef marrow bones for garnish
Chopped fresh tarragon, parsley, chives, and chervil for garnish

Grill the tournedos over the hot coals until medium rare or to taste. Cut them into 4 slices and season with salt and pepper.

Meanwhile, cut the marrow from the bones, slice, and poach it in simmering water to cover for 2 minutes; drain and set aside.

Serving. Arrange the baby vegetables on 2 dinner plates and place a tournedo in the center of each plate. Spoon some of the consommé over all. Serve extra consommé in a sauceboat. Garnish with the marrow and sprinkle with the chopped herbs.

Suggested accompaniments: Small ramekins of cornichons, rock salt, horseradish, Dijon mustard, and pickled cherries.

Fresh Berries with Cassis Sherbet and Champagne

½ cup sugar

1 cup water

1 cinnamon stick

10 fresh mint leaves

1 cup fresh blackberries, raspberries, blueberries,
stemmed strawberries, red currants, or pitted cherries

Cassis Sherbet (recipe follows)

3 or 4 tablespoons champagne

2 mint sprigs

2 slices candied ginger, cut into julienne

In a small saucepan, combine the sugar, water, cinnamon stick, and mint leaves. Bring to a simmer, stirring constantly, until the sugar dissolves. Cover and simmer for 5 minutes. Remove from the heat, uncover, and allow the mixture to cool to room temperature.

Serving. Divide the berries between 2 chilled balloon-shaped goblets and pour a few tablespoons of sugar syrup over them. Top with a scoop of sherbet. Pour the champagne over the sherbet to make some nice looking bubbles. Decorate with the mint and candied ginger and serve at once.

La Colombe d'Or

Cassis Sherbet

1 cup pureéd black currants
1 cup water
½ cup sugar
Juice of 1 lemon
1 egg white
⅛ teaspoon salt

Strain the currant pureé through a fine sieve lined with cheescloth to remove the seeds; set aside.

In a medium saucepan, bring the water and sugar to a simmer but do not boil. Remove from the heat as soon as the sugar has completly dissolved; let cool. Add the currant pureé and lemon juice, and stir over a bowl filled with ice cubes and water until well chilled.

Place in an ice cream machine and partially freeze according to the manufacturer's instructions. Beat the egg white with the salt until stiff peaks form. Fold thoroughly into the half-frozen sherbet. Continue freezing until completely frozen.

La Colombe d'Or

LANGDON HALL

COUNTRY HOUSE HOTEL

Cambridge, Ontario

Langdon House is a grand Colonial Revival—style house designed and built in 1898 to capture the spirit of that gilded age. William Bennett and Mary Beaton discovered Langdon Hall in 1978 and were enchanted by its grandeur and the country way of life. Nearly ten years later they have realized their dream of recreating Langdon Hall as a country house hotel. Langdon Hall recently became a member of Relais & Chateaux.

Langdon Hall is set on forty acres in the heart of Carolinian Canada, a region named for its remarkably mild climate. This narrow strip of land is home to a community of plants different from those found anywhere else in Canada. Guests can enjoy the turn-of-the-century gardens at Langdon Hall, now being restored by one of North America's leading horticulturists.

This country house hotel has peaceful reading rooms and intimate paneled lounges and a bar. All thirty-six bedrooms and seven suites are carefully furnished, and most of the sitting areas are warmed by open fireplaces. Indoors, guests enjoy a billiards and card room and a spa with whirlpool baths, saunas, and exercise and treatment rooms. Outdoors, there is a tennis court, a croquet lawn, a heated swimming pool, horse riding, canoeing, cycling, and, in the winter, cross-country skiing. Nearby is the Stratford Shakespearean Festival Theatre, the Guelph Spring Festival (a month-long celebration of music and the performing arts), the Royal Botanical Gardens, museums, galleries, and antiques shops.

Langdon Hall's elegant dining room offers English and French cuisine. Chef Nigel Didcock, formally trained in England and France, gives a contemporary interpretation to many of the classic dishes. Chef Didcock has created this romantic dinner for two for *Menus and Music*.

141

THE MENU

Langdon Hall

Romance for Two

Goat Cheese Mousseline with Eggplant Confit

*Scallop and Zucchini Towers
with Preserved Lemon Sauce*

*Sliced Veal Sweetbreads on Watercress
with Papaya Salad*

Baked Peaches with Honey-Basil Ice Cream

Goat Cheese Mousseline with Eggplant Confit

Eggplant Confit (recipe follows)
4 ounces fresh goat cheese
1 tablespoon heavy (whipping) cream
1 tablespoon minced fresh parsley, chives, and thyme
Freshly ground pepper to taste
Thyme sprigs for garnish

Prepare the eggplant confit. Just before serving, blend the fresh goat cheese in a small bowl with the cream, minced herbs, and a twist of freshly ground pepper. Mold the goat cheese mixture into 2 olive-shaped quenelles by dipping 2 dessert or soup spoons in hot water and molding the chese with the 2 spoons. Keep the quenelles at room temperature until served.

Serving. Remove the eggplant slices from the marinade and arrange them in the center of 2 plates. The eggplant slices should be slightly overlapping. Reserve the marinade. Place the goat cheese quenelles in the center of the eggplant and spoon some of the marinade around the cheese. Garnish with fresh herbs.

Eggplant Confit

½ onion, sliced

½ tomato, seeded and sliced

1 teaspoon chopped fresh thyme

1 teaspoon chopped fresh rosemary

1 bay leaf

½ teaspoon salt

¼ teaspoon white pepper

1 teaspoon honey

½ cup olive oil

1 garlic clove

2 tablespoons red wine vinegar

1 tablespoon balsamic vinegar

1 tablespoon sherry vinegar

1 Italian eggplant

In a large stainless steel saucepan, combine all the ingredients except the eggplant and simmer them gently over low heat for 10 minutes.

Slice the eggplant into rounds ⅛ inch thick. Add the sliced eggplant to the saucepan and shake the pan so the slices are completely submerged. Simmer for 10 more minutes. Remove from the heat, cool, cover, and marinate in the refrigerator for 2 days.

Note: The eggplant can also be served hot if desired.

Scallop and Zucchini Towers
with Preserved Lemon Sauce

2 large sea scallops, washed and dried
1 zucchini
4 cups water
1 tablespoon butter
2 tablespoons olive oil
Preserved Lemon Sauce (recipe follows)
Fresh lemon thyme leaves to taste
1 peeled, seeded, and diced tomato for garnish
2 lemon thyme sprigs for garnish

Preheat the oven to 300° F. Slice each scallop in thirds crosswise. Score the zucchini skin vertically with a knife and slice into ⅛- to ¼-inch rounds. In a large saucepan or pot, bring the water to a boil and blanch the zucchini for 15 seconds.

In a sauté pan or skillet, melt the butter and fry the scallops on both sides for a total of 2 to 3 minutes. Remove the scallops from the pan. On a baking sheet, build 2 towers by alternating zucchini and scallop layers, starting and ending with zucchini. Drizzle the towers with olive oil and sprinkle with lemon thyme. Bake the towers in the preheated oven for 5 minutes.

Serving. Sprinkle lemon thyme leaves over the warm lemon sauce. Spoon the sauce onto 2 plates. Place a cooked scallop and zucchini tower on top of each. Garnish with the diced tomato and a branch of lemon thyme.

Langdon Hall

Preserved Lemon Sauce

2 shallots, chopped
1 tablespoon butter
1 preserved lemon peel,* diced
2 tablespoons dry white wine
2 tablespoons heavy (whipping) cream
3 tablespoons butter
Chopped fresh chives to taste
Fresh lemon juice to taste

In a sauté pan or skillet, sauté the shallots in butter over medium-high heat until translucent. Add the preserved lemon and white wine to the pan. Boil to reduce the liquid by half and stir in the cream and butter. Adjust the seasoning with chives and lemon juice to taste.

*Remove the rind from 1 lemon. Place the rind in a glass jar with 1 tablespoon of salt and cover with white wine. Seal it and set it aside in a dark, cool place for 3 months.

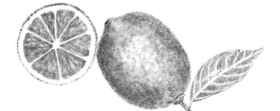

Langdon Hall

Sliced Veal Sweetbreads on
Watercress with Papaya Salad

Papaya Salad

1 green papaya
⅛ teaspoon grated fresh ginger
2 tablespoons minced fresh cilantro
2 tablespoons fresh lime juice
1 shallot, chopped
1 green onion, minced
1 slice smoked veal prosciutto, diced
5 or 6 sliced unblanched almonds, toasted (page 43)

Cut the papaya into thin slices and then into long matchsticks. In a medium bowl, place the papaya, ginger, cilantro, lime juice, shallot, green onion, prosciutto, and almonds. Set this mixture aside to let the flavors blend.

Yogurt Dressing

½ cup plain yogurt
1 teaspoon minced fresh herbs of choice
¼ teaspoon red wine vinegar
Fresh ground white pepper to taste
1 teaspoon peeled, seeded, and diced tomato

In a small bowl, blend the yogurt, herbs, vinegar, pepper, and tomato. Cover and chill the dressing in the refrigerator until ready to serve.

Langdon Hall

Sweetbreads

1 pair veal sweetbreads
Salt and pepper to taste
1 cup flour for dredging
1 egg
1 teaspoon oil
⅛ teaspoon salt
1 cup fresh bread crumbs for coating
1 tablespoon olive oil
1 tablespoon butter
2 bunches watercress, stemmed

Bring a saucepan of water to a boil, add the sweetbreads, and simmer for 5 minutes. Drain the sweetbreads and place them in a bowl of ice water; leave them for several minutes, until they are fully cooled. Use a sharp knife to trim away all the membranes. Pat the sweetbreads dry with paper towels and slice into 4 pieces on a diagonal. Season lightly with salt and pepper. One at a time, dip the slices in the flour, shake off excess flour, then dip in the beaten egg and shake off the excess. Cover with the crumbs and pat until each slice is coated. Pound the sweetbreads with a meat pounder to flatten slightly.

In a large skillet or sauté pan, heat the oil and butter over medium-high heat. Sauté the sweetbreads until lightly browned, about 1 minute on each side. Using a slotted spoon, remove them from the skillet and keep warm until serving.

Serving. Place a bunch of watercress in the center of each of 2 plates. Place the sweetbreads on the watercress. Garnish with the papaya salad, spoon the chilled yogurt dressing over the top, and serve at once.

Langdon Hall

Baked Peaches with Honey-Basil Ice Cream

2 firm ripe peaches
3 tablespoons butter
2 tablespoons honey
1 teaspoon ground cinnamon
¼ cup heavy (whipping) cream
1 bunch basil, stemmed and chopped
1 tablespoon butter
Fresh lemon juice to taste
Honey-Basil Ice Cream (recipe follows)
Basil sprigs and ground cinnamon for garnish

Drop the peaches into boiling water for 10 seconds. Remove the peaches with a slotted spoon and place them in cold water, then peel away the skins. Cut the peaches in half and remove the pits.

Preheat the oven to 350° F. In an ovenproof sauté pan or skillet, heat the butter over high heat; add the peaches and cook until lightly browned. Sprinkle with cinnamon and honey and place the pan in the preheated oven. Bake for 5 to 7 minutes.

Remove the peaches from the pan with a slotted spoon and drain off the excess butter. Return the pan to the heat, add the cream, and bring to a boil. Remove the pan from the heat, add the fresh basil, then incorporate the butter to give the sauce a shine. Add a dash of lemon juice if desired.

Serving. Arrange the peach halves on 2 dessert plates. Spoon the sauce over. Garnish with basil leaves and dust with cinnamon. Serve with the honey-basil ice cream.

Langdon Hall

Honey-Basil Ice Cream

2 cups milk
2 bunches basil, stemmed and chopped
5 egg yolks
⅓ cup sugar
½ cup heavy (whipping) cream
¾ cup honey

In a heavy saucepan, bring the milk and basil just to the boiling point, then remove from the heat. In a mixing bowl, whisk the egg yolks and sugar together until the mixture is a pale yellow. Whisk the egg mixture into the hot milk. Whisking constantly, return the saucepan to moderate heat and cook until the egg and milk mixture gradually thickens and coats the back of a spoon. Do not bring to a simmer or the eggs will curdle.

Remove the pan from the heat and pour the custard into a mixing bowl. Add the cream and honey. Let the mixture stand for 10 minutes to blend the flavors. Strain through a sieve and pour into an ice cream maker. Freeze according to the manufacturer's instructions.

MEADOWOOD RESORT HOTEL

St. Helena, California

Meadowood Resort Hotel is set on 250 acres in the world-famous Napa Valley just north of San Francisco, California. In addition to its Relais & Chateaux membership, Meadowood has received a Four-Star Award from the Mobil Travel Guide and a Four-Diamond Award from the California Automobile Association in 1991. The resort is home for the prestigious Napa Valley Vintners Association and their yearly auction.

Meadowood offers the utmost in relaxation, recreation, and fine lodging. The property includes a nine-hole golf course, championship tennis courts, two croquet courts, a swimming pool, an exercise parcourse, and a wine school. Hikers, cyclists, and joggers enjoy extraordinary natural beauty on trails and paths winding through Meadowood's acres of oak and madrone. Beautifully decorated one-bedroom suites dot the hillsides around the property, each with its own entrance and private deck and most with large stone fireplaces. Rooms are also available in the resort's main lodges.

Much of the excitement in the Napa Valley revolves around wine and food. Meadowood chef Henri Delcros serves a masterful combination of French and California country cuisine at the resort's gracious Starmont Restaurant. He is a winner of the Great Chefs of America Award, and the Starmont Restaurant received the Epicurean Rendezvous Restaurant Award in 1991. An extensive California wine list complements the meals. The San Francisco String Quartet enjoys an association with Meadowood; guests enjoy culinary creations by chef Delcros and concert performances by the San Francisco String Quartet and Friends during the annual Twilight Concerts at Meadowood. Henri Delcros presented *Menus and Music* with the following Napa Valley menu for two.

Meadowood Resort Hotel

THE MENU

Meadowood Resort Hotel

Napa Valley Menu

Asparagus with Cabernet Dressing

Shrimp in Cabbage Leaves with Basil Sauce

Roast Duck with Honey

Strawberries with Champagne Sabayon

Asparagus with Cabernet Dressing

12 medium asparagus spears
Cabernet Dressing (recipe follows)

Wash the asparagus spears and peel them with a small sharp knife. Starting at the butt end, cut down to the tender flesh and peel up to the tip. A vegetable peeler may also be used. Place the asparagus in a steamer basket, and steam, covered, over boiling water until the asparagus are crisp-tender, about 5 minutes. Immediately remove the spears from the pan and drain.

Serving. Arrange the warm asparagus spears on 2 plates and pour the Cabernet dressing over. Serve at room temperature.

Cabernet Dressing

1 whole egg, at room temperature
½ tablespoon Dijon mustard
½ cup olive oil
¼ cup Cabernet wine, at room temperature

In a small bowl, whisk together the egg and mustard. While constantly whipping with the whisk, very slowly add the olive oil until the mixture has thickened to the consistency of mayonnaise. Continue to whip, and add the red wine in a continuous stream, maintaining a thickened sauce.

Note: All ingredients in the Cabernet dressing should be at room temperature before you begin. The dressing may also be made in a blender or food processor.

Meadowood Resort Hotel

Shrimp in Cabbage Leaves with Basil Sauce

½ head Savoy cabbage
8 colossal or jumbo shrimp*
Salt and pepper to taste
Basil Sauce (recipe follows)

Core and wash the leaves of the Savoy cabbage. Choose 4 of the largest leaves. Bring a saucepan of water to a boil, then add the cabbage leaves. Cook until crisp-tender, about 5 minutes. Remove the leaves promptly and rinse under cold water. Drain on a towel.

Peel and devein the shrimp. Place them in a steamer basket over an inch of boiling water. Cover and steam for 2 to 3 minutes. Place 2 shrimp in the center of each cabbage leaf, season lightly with salt and pepper, and wrap into a small package. Place the packages of cabbage-wrapped shrimp in the steamer basket over boiling water. Cover and heat for 2 minutes.

Serving. Place the cabbage-wrapped shrimp on 2 serving plates and pour some of the basil sauce over.

*Chef Delcros uses Santa Barbara shrimp, which are extremely large (10 to 15 per pound). These are preferred if you can find them.

Basil Sauce

⅓ cup minced shallots
2 large garlic cloves, crushed
½ bunch basil, stemmed and minced
2 tablespoons minced fresh tarragon
2 tablespoons minced fresh chervil or parsley
½ cup virgin olive oil
Salt and pepper to taste

In a mixing bowl, combine the shallots, garlic, basil, tarragon, and chervil or parsley. Mix in the olive oil. Season with salt and pepper. Set aside.

Note: This sauce also is excellent warmed in a small saucepan over low heat just before serving.

Roast Duck with Honey

1 tablespoon softened butter
1 tablespoon flour
2 half breasts Muscovy duck
¼ cup honey
2 tablespoons red wine vinegar
2 cups dry red wine

Preheat the oven to 250° F. In a small ovenproof pan, make a roux by combining the butter and flour, then baking this mixture in the preheated oven for 15 minutes, or until golden brown.

Raise the oven temperature to 400° F. Place the duck breasts in a roasting pan and bake in the preheated oven until golden brown, about 10 minutes.

In a heavy 1-quart pot, cook and stir the honey over high heat until the honey is thick and golden brown, being careful not to burn it. Add the red wine vinegar and cook and stir until it thickens again. Add the red wine and simmer until reduced by half, about 15 minutes. Add the roux and stir the sauce until it thickens. Strain the sauce through a sieve.

Serving. Arrange the duck breasts on 2 serving plates and pour the warm honey sauce over the duck.

Strawberries with Champagne Sabayon

2 egg yolks
¼ cup heavy (whipping) cream
1 tablespoon sugar
½ cup Brut champagne
1 cup strawberries, rinsed, drained, and hulled

In a stainless steel pan, combine the yolks, cream, sugar, and champagne. Over low heat, whisk the ingredients until they thicken enough to coat the back of a spoon. Remove from the heat and serve warm, tepid, or chilled.

Serving. Place the strawberries in 2 wine glasses or on dessert plates and spoon the champagne sabayon over.

THE MILLCROFT INN

Alton, Ontario

The Millcroft Inn is a beautifully restored nineteenth-century knitting mill that has been transformed into an award-winning inn. Nestled on one hundred acres of rolling Caledon Hills, it is situated next to a huge pond and waterfall and built of Inglewood Quarry stone and warm Georgia pine. The Millcroft Inn is a member of Relais & Chateaux.

The Mill's twenty-two newly refurbished guest rooms are decorated with a blend of European and Canadian antiques. Behind the Inn and across the falls are twenty contemporary two-story chalets. The Manor House, formerly the mill owner's residence, has been recently restored and now holds nine luxurious bedrooms with hot tubs and fireplaces.

Guests at the Inn can enjoy peaceful strolls along country paths, boating on the millpond, tennis, morning hot-air-balloon rides, and bicycling, as well as relaxing in the heated pool, saunas, and whirlpool baths. In the winter, there is cross-country skiing and snowshoeing in the surrounding hills, and downhill skiing nearby.

The Inn offers sumptuous dining and selections from an extensive wine cellar to be savored in the timbered dining room or in a romantic glass pod suspended over the falls. The Millcroft Inn's chef Fredy Stamm created the following menu and recipes and presented them to *Menus and Music*.

THE MENU

The Millcroft Inn

Cream of Artichoke Soup with Smoked Salmon

Warm Chicken Salad with Rosemary Dressing

Champagne and Tarragon Sherbet

Poached Beef Fillets with Horseradish and Mint Sauce

Peppered Strawberries

The Millcroft Inn

Cream of Artichoke Soup with Smoked Salmon

5 poached artichoke bottoms (recipe follows)
2 tablespoons butter
2 tablespoons diced raw potato
⅓ cup champagne
4 cups Chicken Stock (page 220) or canned chicken broth
1 cup heavy (whipping) cream
2 tablespoons butter, softened
1 ounce smoked salmon, cut into julienne, for garnish

Prepare the artichoke bottoms. In a medium saucepan, melt the butter and sauté the artichoke bottoms and potato over medium-high heat for 5 minutes. Add the champagne and chicken stock or broth and simmer for 20 minutes. Remove from the heat and let cool. Transfer to a blender or food processor and purée until smooth, then force through a fine sieve into a medium saucepan, pressing the vegetables with the back of a spoon.

Stir in the cream and bring the soup to a boil. Reduce to a simmer and cook for 15 minutes. Remove from the heat and whisk in the softened butter. Ladle immediately into 2 bowls and garnish with smoked salmon julienne.

Note: This soup chills beautifully. Follow the instructions above, omitting the softened butter. Allow the soup to cool before refrigerating overnight. Serve in chilled bowls and garnish with smoked salmon julienne.

Artichoke Bottoms

5 large artichokes
5 cups water
¼ cup fresh lemon juice
½ teaspoon salt

The Millcroft Inn

Slice the stems off the base of the artichokes. Snap off the outer leaves by pulling them back, then cut off the remaining cone of leaves on top. Brush cut portions with lemon juice to prevent discoloration. In a stainless steel or enameled pan, simmer the artichoke bottoms in the water, lemon juice, and salt for 30 to 40 minutes, or until they are very tender when pierced with a sharp knife. Let them cool, then refrigerate in the cooking liquid until needed.

Shortly before using the artichoke bottoms, wash them under cold water and scoop out the choke with a teaspoon. Trim off any tough leaf ends.

Note: The artichoke bottoms can be prepared in advance, and will keep in the liquid for 2 or 3 days in the refrigerator.

The Millcroft Inn

Warm Chicken Salad with Rosemary Dressing

Celery Onion Marinade

2 tablespoons julienne-cut celery root
¼ red onion, finely sliced
3 tablespoons olive oil
Salt and pepper to taste
Juice of ½ lemon

In a mixing bowl, combine the celery root and onion; toss with the olive oil, lemon juice, salt, and pepper. Marinate for at least 10 minutes, or cover and refrigerate until needed.

Note: This marinade can be prepared several days in advance and kept, covered, in the refrigerator.

Chicken Salad

1 whole chicken breast, halved, boned, and skinned
Salt, pepper, and paprika to taste
1 teaspoon olive oil
1 tablespoon butter
Leaves from ½ head Boston lettuce

Season the chicken breasts with salt, pepper, and paprika. In a sauté pan or skillet, heat the butter and olive oil over medium-low heat and slowly sauté the chicken breasts until medium rare, about 3 minutes on each side. Remove the breasts from the pan and keep them warm until serving. Set the pan with its juices aside.

Serving. Divide the Boston lettuce leaves between 2 salad plates and top with the celery and onion marinade. Cut the chicken breasts into long strips and arrange over the lettuce. Drizzle with the rosemary dressing and serve immediately.

The Millcroft Inn

Rosemary Dressing

½ teaspoon chopped shallots
Leaves from 2 rosemary sprigs, chopped
3 tablespoons Vegetable Broth (page 227)
3 tablespoons olive oil
2 tablespoons sherry vinegar
Salt and pepper to taste

In the pan containing the juices from the chicken, add the shallots and rosemary and cook over high heat for 30 seconds. Deglaze the pan with the vegetable broth and continue cooking to reduce the sauce to one third its original volume. Remove the pan from the heat and let cool to room temperature. Whisk in the vinegar, then the olive oil. Season with salt and pepper.

The Millcroft Inn

Champagne and Tarragon Sherbet

¾ cup sugar
1 ⅓ cups water
1 teaspoon chopped fresh tarragon
2 cups champagne
1 tablespoon fresh lemon juice
1 egg white

In a medium saucepan, combine the sugar, water, and tarragon and bring to a boil. Add the champagne and lemon juice. Let cool and freeze for 30 minutes in an ice cream machine following the manufacturer's instructions. In a medium bowl, beat the egg white until stiff and fold into the sherbet. Return the sherbet to the freezer for 30 minutes, or until frozen.

Serving. The moment before serving, scoop a ball or two of the sherbert into each of 2 chilled goblets.

Note: This will serve 4 people as a palate refresher, or 2 as a wonderful summer dessert.

The Millcroft Inn

Poached Beef Fillets with Horseradish and Mint Sauce

1 ⅓ cups Vegetable Broth (page 227)
Two 5-ounce beef fillet steaks
Horseradish and Mint Sauce (recipe follows)

In a medium saucepan, bring the vegetable broth to a boil. Poach the steaks until medium rare, or until the meat springs back when pressed with your finger. Remove the steaks with a slotted spoon, cover, and keep warm until serving; reserve the vegetable broth. Prepare the horseradish and mint suace.

Serving. Ladle the warm horseradish mint sauce onto 2 plates. Slice each warm fillet into 4 thin slices and arrange them on the sauce. Garnish with mint sprigs.

Horseradish and Mint Sauce

Reserved vegetable broth from the above recipe
⅔ cup heavy (whipping) cream
1 teaspoon grated prepared horseradish, or
½ teaspoon grated fresh horseradish
1 tablespoon butter, softened
Leaves from 2 mint sprigs, chopped
Salt and pepper to taste
Mint sprigs for garnish

In a small, heavy saucepan, cook the reserved vegetable broth over very high heat until the liquid reduces to 2 or 3 tablespoons. Stir in the cream and the horseradish, and boil to reduce until the sauce thickens enough to coat the back of a spoon. Remove from the heat and whisk the butter into the sauce. Fold in the chopped mint and season to taste.

The Millcroft Inn

Peppered Strawberries

2 cups strawberries
2 ½ teaspoons sugar
2 teaspoons kirsch
2 teaspoons Grand Marnier
Freshly ground black pepper to taste
⅓ cup heavy (whipping) cream
2 scoops strawberry ice cream
2 mint leaves

Hull, wash, and quarter the strawberries. In a medium bowl, mix the strawberries with the sugar, kirsch, and Grand Marnier. Macerate for 15 minutes. Dust the berries generously with black pepper, turning the pepper mill 2 or 3 times, and set aside.

Whip the heavy cream until soft peaks form. In a mixing bowl, whisk the ice cream until soft and fold in the whipped cream. Carefully fold in the berries and their macerating liquid.

Serving. Immediately place the berries in 2 glass bowls or tall glasses and garnish each serving with a mint leaf. Serve at once.

The Millcroft Inn

THE POINT

Saranac Lake, New York

The Point was originally the home of William A. Rockefeller and was the last and most lavish of the Adirondack Great Camps. Set on New York's Upper Suranac Lake, The Point continues the tradition of sumptuous Adirondack retreats by offering guests warm hospitality in a rustic and luxurious atmosphere. It recaptures the gracious lifestyle of a private home from a bygone era, with eleven distinctive guest quarters that have been beautifully appointed and meticulously restored by owners Christie and David Garrett.

There are no organized activites at The Point, but guests can explore the lake in antique boats, hike through the woods, fish, swim, and water ski; play croquet, badminton, or horseshoes; or enjoy lunch under the pines. Winter activities include cross-country skiing, skating on the lake, ice fishing, and skiing the Olympic slopes at nearby Lake Placid.

The resort's Great Hall, with its enormous stone fireplaces, massive wood beams, and deep couches, continues the tradition of elegant Great Camp dining. The imaginative Continental cuisine gains an Adirondack accent from the use of fresh vegetables, game, and fish. All dinners and lunches are served at round tables in the Great Hall unless other arrangements are made. As in a private home, there is no menu selection, but the fine food and wine always make meals at the Point a very special event. The following menu and recipes were prepared for *Menus and Music* by The Point's chef, Neil Wigglesworth.

THE MENU

The Point

Oysters with Truffled Asparagus and Wild Mushrooms

Roasted Rabbit with Vermouth Sauce

Raspberry Millefeuille

Oysters with Truffled Asparagus
and Wild Mushrooms

6 oysters in their shells
½ cup (1 stick) butter
1 bunch thin asparagus, trimmed
1 ounce black truffle, sliced
1 ounce chanterelles
1 ounce morels
1 ounce cèpes
3 shallots, minced
¼ cup heavy (whipping) cream
Pepper to taste
Blanched seaweed for garnish

Preheat the oven to 350° F. Shuck the oysters over a bowl, reserving their juices.
Rinse each oyster's deepest shell and set the oysters and deep shells aside.
Cut the asparagus spears in half lengthwise, and then into 1-inch pieces. In a sauté
pan or skillet, melt half the butter over medium heat and sauté the asparagus,
turning the stalks often, until cooked through but still crisp, about 2 to 3 minutes.
Remove the pan from the heat and add the truffles. Set aside.

Trim, wash and pat the mushrooms dry, then chop them into a small dice. In a
sauté pan or skillet, heat the remaining 4 tablespoons of the butter and sauté the
mushrooms and shallots until the shallots are translucent, about 3 to 5 minutes.
Stir in the cream and continue cooking until the mixture thickens enough to coat a
spoon. Season with pepper and keep warm until serving.

In a small saucepan, gently heat the reserved oyster juice and the oysters until
warmed through. Briefly warm the oyster shells in the oven.

Serving. Place some blanched seaweed on each of 2 serving plates, and arrange 3
warm oyster shells on top of each. Spoon a little of the warm mushroom mixture
into each shell and place the oysters on top. Arrange the asparagus and truffle
mixture over the oysters.

Roasted Rabbit with Vermouth Sauce

One 2- to 3-pound rabbit

Remove the fillets from the rabbit. Remove the back legs, debone the legs, then tie the legs in 3 places with cotton string to retain their shape while cooking. Refrigerate the fillets and legs until 30 minutes before cooking. Reserve the rabbit carcass for the rabbit glace.

Rabbit Glace

1 rabbit carcass (reserved from roasted rabbit, above)
2 tablespoons butter
½ medium onion, chopped
1 carrot, peeled and chopped
1 stalk celery, chopped
1 leek, chopped
½ cup dry white wine
4 cups Veal Stock (page 226) or reduced canned chicken broth

Preheat the oven to 350° F. Chop the rabbit carcass into small pieces and roast in the oven for 20 minutes or until golden brown. In a large, heavy saucepan, melt the butter and sauté the chopped onion, carrot, celery, and leek until the vegetables are tender. Add the rabbit carcass, white wine, and veal stock or chicken broth and simmer for 2½ hours, adding water as needed so that ingredients are always covered. Strain the stock through a sieve and return to the heat, cooking until the stock reduces to the consistency of a syrup. Cool and refrigerate.

Note: Freeze unused glace in a covered container.

Vermouth Sauce

2 tablespoons butter
6 shallots, minced
2 cups dry white vermouth
1 ½ cups dry white wine
½ cup heavy (whipping) cream
¼ cup rabbit glace, above
1 tomato

In a sauté pan or skillet, melt the butter over medium-high heat and sauté the shallots until translucent. Add the vermouth and white wine and reduce the liquid by three fourths. Stir in the cream and reduce the liquid again by half. Whisk in the rabbit glace. In a saucepan, place the tomato in boiling water to cover and blanch for 30 seconds. Remove with a slotted spoon and cool. Peel the tomato, then cut it in half and squeeze to remove the seeds. Mince the tomato and set it aside.

Cooking and Serving the Rabbit

2 tablespoons butter
3 carrots, peeled and cut into very thin 1-inch strips
4 celery stalks, peeled and cut into very thin 1-inch strips
4 ounces pasta
2 chives, chopped
2 thyme sprigs for garnish

Remove the rabbit from the refrigerator 30 minutes before cooking. Preheat the oven to 350° F. Place the back legs of the rabbit in a roasting pan and bake for 10 to 20 minutes. Allow to rest for 10 minutes, then remove the string and slice. Meanwhile, in a sauté pan or skillet, melt the butter and sauté the fillets, turning to coat all sides with butter. Cook for 4 to 6 minutes, until golden. Allow to rest for 10 minutes, then slice.

Meanwhile, pour enough water in a pot to cover the carrots and celery and heat until boiling. Add the carrots and celery, cover, and gently boil for about 3 minutes, or until crisp-tender. Drain and set aside.

In a 6-quart kettle, bring 3 to 4 quarts of salted water to a rolling boil, add the pasta, and boil until al dente; drain.

Stir the chopped chives and the minced tomato into the warm vermouth sauce. Divide the pasta between 2 dinner plates. Arrange the rabbit legs and filets on top of the pasta, and spoon the vermouth sauce over. Garnish the plate with carrots, celery, and thyme sprigs.

Raspberry Millefeuille

2 baskets fresh raspberries
Two 7-inch circles puff pastry*
¼ cup Pastry Cream (recipe follows)
Sugar to taste
Whipped cream for garnish
6 mint leaves
Sifted powdered sugar

Rinse and drain the raspberries; set aside.

Preheat the oven to 350° F. On a large baking sheet covered with parchment or greased with butter, place the pastry circles and bake in the preheated oven until golden brown, about 8 minutes. Allow to cool, then cut in half crosswise.

Serving. Spread the raspberry purée over the bottom halves of the pastry circles; spread a layer of pastry cream over the purée. Pipe a border of whipped cream around the edge of the pastries, and place the whole raspberries in the center on top of the pastry cream. Cut the mint leaves into fine strips and sprinkle them over the fruit. Place the pastry lids on top of the fruit and dust with powdered sugar. Pour the remaining raspberry coulis onto 2 dessert plates and place the puff pastries on top.

*Use the puff pastry recipe on page 191, or defrosted frozen puff pastry.

Pastry Cream

3 egg yolks
¼ cup sugar
1 ½ tablespoons flour
1 cup plus 2 tablespoons milk
½ vanilla bean, split

In a medium bowl, whisk together the egg yolks and 1 tablespoon of the sugar, and whisk until the yolks are thick and pale. Sift in the flour and mix well. In a small saucepan, place the milk, the remaining 3 tablespoons of the sugar, and the vanilla bean and bring to a boil. Remove from heat and whisk into the egg mixture. Transfer the mixture back into the saucepan, and cook over low heat until it thickens enough to coat the back of a spoon. Remove from heat. Remove the vanilla bean before serving.

SAN YSIDRO RANCH

Montecito, California

The San Ysidro Ranch is nestled in the foothills of the San Ynez Mountains overlooking the Pacific Ocean near Santa Barbara, California. Originally part of a Spanish land grant and the California mission system, San Ysidro Ranch has welcomed guests since 1893. Actor Ronald Colman bought San Ysidro in 1935 and made it a favorite hideaway for celebrities such as Lawrence Olivier, John and Jacqueline Kennedy, Paul Newman and Joanne Woodward, and Mick Jagger. The San Ysidro Ranch offers privacy, warm service, country comfort, and an inspiring natural setting. Secluded cottages share the main grounds with hundred-year-old trees and wide terraces of flowers, citrus trees, the chef's herb garden, and lawns. Guests enjoy guided horseback riding on trails over the ranch's 540 acres, tennis on three courts, hiking with spectacular ocean and mountain views, or simply lounging by the heated pool. San Ysidro Ranch is a member of Relais & Chateaux.

Dining at San Ysidro is a special treat. Chef Mark Ehrler takes full advantage of California's famous seafood, produce, and wines to create contemporary dishes with a French accent. Chef Ehrler created the following romantic menu and recipes for *Menus and Music.*

San Ysidro Ranch

THE MENU

San Ysidro Ranch

A Romantic Evening for Two

Smoked Salmon Tart with a Sprinkle of Salmon Caviar

Maine Lobster and Crunchy Vegetable Salad

Chilled Champagne and Grapefruit Soup

Loin of Lamb with Mango Sauce and Peas

Salad of Fried Goat Cheese Ravioli

Hazelnut Parfait with Espresso Sauce

San Ysidro Ranch

Smoked Salmon Tart with a Sprinkle of Salmon Caviar

Two 4-inch circles puff pastry, * *⅛ inch thick*
¼ cup heavy (whipping) cream
Fresh lemon juice to taste
Salt and pepper to taste
1 ounce (2 tablespoons) salmon caviar
1 tablespoon minced fresh chives
6 ounces sliced smoked salmon

Preheat the oven to 350° F for at least 20 minutes. Place the puff pastry on a baking sheet and place a rack or baking sheet on top of them to keep them from rising too high while baking. Bake in the preheated oven until they are nicely puffed and brown and the sides are crisp, about 15 to 20 minutes. Remove and let cool to room temperature.

In a deep bowl, whip the cream until firm. Gently stir in the lemon juice, salt, pepper, half the salmon caviar, and the chives.

Serving. Spread a thin layer of the cream sauce over each puff pastry. Arrange the salmon slices on top in a flower shape. Place each pastry on a plate and spoon some of the sauce around the pastry. Sprinkle with the rest of the salmon caviar.

*See page 191 for homemade puff pastry, or use defrosted frozen puff pastry.

San Ysidro Ranch

Maine Lobster and Crunchy Vegetable Salad

Two 1-pound lobsters
3 quarts salted water
1 large tomato
1 jumbo white mushroom
4 thin asparagus spears
6 fava bean pods
1 tablespoon fresh lemon juice
Salt and pepper to taste
1 tablespoon truffle juice
2 tablespoons extra-virgin olive oil

With cotton string, tie the lobsters together with their stomachs touching and their tails straight. In a large pot, bring the water to a boil. Plunge the lobsters in, return to a boil, and cook for 8 minutes. Remove the lobsters from the pot and cool them in a pan of ice water. Remove the shells from the tail, claws, and knuckles, cut through the underside of the tail, and remove the tail meat in large pieces. Set aside.

Dice the tomato into small cubes and reserve. Cut the mushroom in half and thinly slice. Beginning at the tips, slice the asparagus spears at an angle to make thin shavings. Shuck the fava beans and blanch them in salted boiling water for 30 seconds; remove with a slotted spoon. Remove the skin from the beans and split the beans in half.

In a medium ceramic or glass bowl, whisk together the lemon juice, salt, pepper, truffle juice, and olive oil. Add all the vegetables, season again with salt and pepper to taste, and marinate for about 30 minutes. Strain the vegetables and reserve the marinade.

San Ysidro Ranch

Serving. Place the vegetable mixture in a mound in the center of each serving plate. Arrange the lobster tail medallions at the bottom of the vegetable mound in the shape of a flower, with the red part of the meat showing on the outside of the plate. Place the lobster tail at the base of the plate. Take the 2 claws and cross them together at the top of the plate. Place the knuckles over the vegetable mound. Pour the reserved marinade over the lobsters and serve.

Chilled Champagne and Grapefruit Soup

1 large grapefruit, peeled and cut into segments
12 cantaloupe balls, made with a small melon baller
Dry champagne
6 small mint leaves

Serving. Divide the grapefruit segments between 2 chilled soup bowls, arranging them in a flower shape. Place 6 cantaloupe balls in the center of each grapefruit flower. Pour champagne very slowly into the prepared bowls and sprinkle 3 mint leaves into each.

Note: The fruit may be prepared and arranged in advance and chilled. Add the champagne the moment before serving.

Loin of Lamb with Mango Sauce and Peas

2 cups dry red wine
¼ cup brandy
1 tablespoon red wine vinegar
1 tablespoon olive oil
3 thyme sprigs
2 garlic cloves
One 1-pound boneless loin of lamb
½ cup shelled fresh peas
1 tablespoon butter
Salt and freshly ground pepper to taste
Mango Sauce (recipe follows)

Combine the red wine, brandy, vinegar, olive oil, thyme, and garlic in a non-aluminum pan large enough to hold the loin of lamb. Add the lamb and marinate in the refrigerator, covered, for 12 hours, turning occasionally. Remove the lamb from the marinade, and reserve the marinade for the mango sauce.

Preheat the oven to 375° F. In a sauté pan or skillet, brown the lamb in 2 tablespoons of the butter; then transfer it to a baking pan and roast in the preheated oven until medium rare, about 20 minutes, or to your preference. Meanwhile, in a medium saucepan cook the peas in boiling salted water until just tender, about 10 minutes, then drain and set aside. In a sauté pan or skillet, melt the butter and sauté the peas until warm. Season with salt and pepper.

Serving. Place the peas on the upper part of each plate. Slice the lamb and fan the slices around the peas. Pour the mango sauce over the meat.

Mango Sauce

Reserved lamb marinade from above recipe
1 mango, peeled, seeded, and cut into chunks
1 tablespoon butter
Salt and pepper to taste

Strain the lamb marinade. In a saucepan, bring the marinade to a boil over high heat and reduce it by two thirds. Add the mango and bring the mixture to a boil while blending together. Whip the butter into the sauce and add the salt and pepper. Remove from the heat.

San Ysidro Ranch

Salad of Fried Goat Cheese Ravioli

Six 3½-inch-square wonton wrappers
1 egg yolk, beaten
3 slices goat cheese
6 small basil leaves
Freshly ground pepper to taste
Vegetable oil for deep-frying
2 handfuls mixed baby lettuces
1 tablespoon balsamic vinegar
2 tablespoons olive oil

Place the 6 wonton wrappers next to each other on a work surface. Brush a ½-inch border around each side with the egg yolk. Cut each slice of goat cheese in half and lay each on a half portion of each wonton wrapper. Place a basil leaf and a dash of black pepper on each cheese slice. Close the wrappers over the cheese and basil and press together at the edges.

In a heavy skillet or a wok, preheat the oil to 325° F degrees. Fry the ravioli for 3 to 5 minutes, or until light golden brown. Drain on paper towels.

Serving. Arrange the lettuces on 2 plates and place 3 ravioli on top of each bed. Sprinkle with the balsamic vinegar and olive oil and serve at once.

Hazelnut Parfait with Espresso Sauce

1 cup sugar
¼ cup water
6 egg yolks
½ cup toasted hazelnuts, ground (page 225)
1 teaspoon Frangelica (hazelnut liqueur)
2 cups heavy whipping cream
Espresso Sauce (recipe follows)

In a small heavy saucepan, cook the sugar and water until the mixture reaches 250° F on a candy thermometer. In a deep bowl, beat the egg yolks with an electric mixer. As the yolks blend, slowly pour in the sugar-water mixture. The yolks will become whiter and lighter. Beat until the egg mixture is cold, then fold in the hazelnuts and Frangelica.

In another deep bowl, whip the cream until it forms stiff peaks. Fold the cream into the egg mixture. Pour into 2 ramekins and freeze for 4 hours.

Serving. Unmold the parfaits onto 2 plates and surround with the espresso sauce.

San Ysidro Ranch

Espresso Sauce

3 egg yolks

1 cup milk

⅓ cup sugar

2 tablespoons freshly ground espresso beans

In a mixing bowl, beat the egg yolks until frothy. In a small saucepan, bring the milk and sugar just to the boiling point; then pour over the eggs and blend. Return this mixture to the saucepan and cook over medium-high heat without allowing to boil. Stir with a wooden spoon until the mixture is thick enough to coat the back of the spoon. Remove from the heat and immediately add the ground espresso beans. Let the mixture infuse for about 10 minutes. Strain through a fine sieve or a double layer of cheesecloth.

Makes about 1½ cups

San Ysidro Ranch

SHERMAN HOUSE

San Francisco, California

The Sherman House was originally built in 1876 for Leander Sherman, founder of the Sherman and Clay Music Company, in San Francisco, California. The Pacific Heights mansion flourished for nearly three decades at the center of the literary, musical, and artistic life of the city. The focus of attention was a three-story music recital hall where the greats of the music world performed; Enrico Caruso, Victor Herbert, Ignace Jan Paderewski, and Edward MacDowell were among the frequent prominent guests. The Sherman House was designated as a historic landmark in 1972.

Manouchehr and Vesta Mobedshahi purchased the Sherman House in 1980 and have restored the property to its original grandeur, recreating it as a small world-class hotel. The hotel has been splendidly refurbished by renowned interior designer William Gaylord, who selected fine art and antique furnishings for the hotel's rooms and suites. The gardens of this urban sanctuary, originally designed by Thomas Church, cover a third of an acre and include a Victorian greenhouse imported from England. The carriage house now holds three suites. The Sherman House is a member of Relais & Chateaux.

Dining at the Sherman House is like being a privileged guest in the finest private home. The evening meals blend fine classical French and Californian cuisine. The Sherman House has a long history of involvement with music and the performing arts, and the combination of their Saint Valentine's dinner menu with beautiful music is a perfect match. Sherman House chef Donia Bijan created the following menu and recipes.

THE MENU

The Sherman House

Saint Valentine's Day Dinner

*Warm Scallop Salad
with a Blush of Blood Orange Vinaigrette*

Cream of Sorrel Soup with Frazzled Potatoes

Passionfruit Sorbet

Roast Duck Breast with Sour Cherries

Bread and Cheese

Napoleon of Forbidden Fruit

Warm Scallop Salad with a Blush of Blood Orange Vinaigrette

2 handfuls mixed greens such as frisée, arugula, and oakleaf lettuce
¼ pound sea scallops
1 tablespoon olive oil
Blood Orange Vinaigrette (recipe follows)
Sections of blood oranges for garnish

Wash the salad greens, dry well, and set aside.

Wash the scallops in cold water and pat them dry with paper towels. Keep the scallops refrigerated until the moment of cooking. Set a sauté pan or skillet over high heat and add the olive oil. Quickly sauté the scallops on both sides until they are just opaque, a total of 2 or 3 minutes. Remove from heat and set aside.

Toss the salad greens with most of the vinaigrette until all the leaves are lightly coated. Reserve 3 tablespoons of the vinaigrette for the scallops.

Serving. Divide the greens between 2 salad plates and place the warm scallops on top. Brush the scallops with the remaining vinaigrette. If you wish, garnish the salad with sections of blood oranges.

Blood Orange Vinaigrette

½ cup virgin olive oil
Juice from 3 blood oranges
½ shallot, minced
Salt and pepper to taste

Whisk together the olive oil, orange juice, shallot, salt, and pepper until thoroughly combined.

The Sherman House

Cream of Sorrel Soup with Frazzled Potatoes

1 tablespoon butter
5 shallots, chopped
3 cups sorrel, stemmed
2 cups Chicken Stock (page 220) or canned chicken broth
1 cup heavy (whipping) cream
Salt and pepper to taste
Frazzled Potatoes (recipe follows)

In a medium saucepan, melt the butter and sauté the shallots until translucent. Add the sorrel and stir until it just wilts, then add the chicken stock or broth. Bring to a boil, then remove from the heat. Transfer to a blender or food processor and purée. Strain through a sieve back into the saucepan. Add the cream, salt, and pepper. Reheat but do not simmer for too long or the soup will lose its color.

Serving. Ladle the warm soup into 2 serving bowls and gently place the hot potatoes on top.

Frazzled Potatoes

1 russet potato, peeled
½ cup peanut oil
Salt to taste

Finely julienne the potato. In a sauté pan or skillet, heat the oil until very hot and fry the potatoes until golden. Drain them on paper towels and sprinkle with salt. Serve at once.

The Sherman House

Passionfruit Sorbet

½ pound passionfruit
1 cup water
½ cup sugar
2 mint sprigs

Cut the passionfruit in half and scoop out the pulp. In a blender or food processor, purée the passionfruit pulp and strain through a sieve; set aside.

In a small saucepan, combine the water and sugar and bring to a boil, mixing so the sugar thoroughly dissolves. Remove the pan from heat and let cool to room temperature. Whisk the syrup into the passionfruit purée. Pour the mixture into an ice cream maker and freeze according to the manufacturer's instructions.

Serving. Place a scoop or two of sorbet in each of 2 chilled glasses and garnish each with a sprig of mint.

The Sherman House

Roast Duck Breast with Sour Cherries

Two single Peking duck breasts, or 1 single Muscovy drake breast
Salt and pepper to taste
¼ cup cassis (black currant) liqueur
1 cup Duck Stock (page 221) or reduced canned chicken broth
1 cup dried sour cherries, pitted

Preheat the oven to 400° F. If you have a whole duck you may remove the breasts and use the rest to make the duck stock. Season the duck breasts with salt and pepper. Heat an ovenproof sauté pan or skillet over high heat until very hot. Place the duck breasts skin side down in the pan. When the skin turns golden, place the pan in the oven and finish cooking the duck breasts until the meat turns pink, about 8 to 10 minutes. Remove the pan from the oven. Remove the duck breasts and set aside.

Pour off the fat from the roasting pan and return the pan to the stove. Deglaze the pan with the cassis liqueur and duck stock or chicken broth. Cook over medium-high heat to reduce the liquid by half. Add the cherries, simmer for 1 minute, and season with salt and pepper.

Serving. Slice the duck breasts and place on 2 warm dinner plates. Pour the sauce over the duck.

The Sherman House

Napoleon of Forbidden Fruit

Puff Pastry*

½ cup (1 stick) cold butter, cut into small cubes
1 cup plus ½ tablespoon unbleached all-purpose flour
½ teaspoon salt
¼ cup ice water

In a medium bowl, with a pastry cutter or 2 knives cut the butter into the flour and salt until crumbly, or process for 10 seconds in a food processor. Sprinkle in the water and mix with a fork, then press together to form a ball (or process for 20 seconds in a food processor); do not knead or overmix. Refrigerate for at least 1 hour before rolling out.

On a lightly floured surface, roll out the dough into a 6-by-12-inch rectangle. Fold the ends of the dough over in thirds like a letter to make 3 layers. Refrigerate for 1 hour. Roll out the pastry and repeat the triple fold 3 more times, refrigerating the dough between each turn. After the fourth turn, roll out the dough into a 6-by-12-inch rectangle.

Preheat the oven to 400° F for at least 20 minutes. Cover a baking sheet with parchment paper or grease with butter, and place the puff pastry on top. Place another piece of parchment on top and cover with a second baking sheet, or butter the second baking sheet and invert it over the puff pastry. Bake in the preheated oven for 25 minutes, or until golden brown. Cool the pastry and cut with a serrated knife into six 2-by-4-inch rectangles.

*Rather than making your own, you could use 1 sheet of defrosted frozen puff pastry.

The Sherman House

Apple Filling

4 tablespoons butter
3 Golden Delicious apples, peeled, cored, and diced
2 tablespoons honey

In a sauté pan or skillet, melt the butter and sauté the apples until golden. Add the honey; cook and stir until the mixture is thickened.

Vanilla Cream

½ cup sour cream
½ heavy (whipping) cream
½ vanilla bean

Place the sour cream and heavy cream into a deep bowl. Grate the vanilla bean into the mixture, then beat the mixture until soft peaks form.

Caramel Sauce

½ cup sugar
¼ cup water
¼ cup heavy (whipping) cream

Place the sugar and water in a heavy saucepan and cook over high heat until the mixture turns golden brown; watch carefully to keep it from burning. Remove the pan from heat and whisk in the heavy cream until fully incorporated.

Note: This sauce can be prepared up to a week in advance and kept refrigerated.

The Sherman House

Assembling and Garnishing

Prepared caramel sauce
Prepared puff pastry
Prepared fillings
Sifted powdered sugar for topping

Spoon some of the caramel sauce onto 2 dessert plates. Place 1 layer of pastry in the center of each and top with a spoonful of the vanilla cream and a spoonful of apple filling. Place a second layer of pastry on top and repeat with the apples and cream. Cover with a third layer of pastry and sift powdered sugar over.

The Sherman House

TIMBERHILL RANCH

Cazadero, California

Timberhill Ranch is a world of utter tranquility set on eighty acres above Timber Cove on the Sonoma coast, three hours north of San Francisco, California. This serene ridgetop hideaway, with its breathtaking views of high meadows, gentle ponds, and redwood-dotted hillsides, includes a main lodge and ten very comfortable guest cottages. The property includes world-class tennis courts, a swimming pool, an outdoor Jacuzzi, and six thousand acres of hiking trails on park land adjacent to the resort. Timberhill recently became a member of the prestigious Relais & Chateaux Association and was distinguished with the Mobil Travel Guide Four-Star Award for 1991.

Exquisite six-course dinners are savored in the dining room of Timberhill's main lodge at candlelit tables for two. There is an outstanding selection of Sonoma, Napa, and Mendocino County wines to complement the dinner. The restaurant's daily-changing menu emphasizes fresh local ingredients as well as homemade breads, pastries, and desserts. Timberhill, a labor of love, is home to the four hosts who own and manage it with style and grace: Barbara L. Farell, Tarran K. McDaid, Michael G. Riordan, and Franklin W. Watson.

THE MENU

Timberhill Ranch

Sweet Red Pepper Bisque

Steamed Salmon and Asparagus with Orange Sauce

Roasted Breast of Pheasant with Ginger Sesame Glaze

Spiced Pears with Rum-Caramel Sauce

Sweet Red Pepper Bisque

4 red bell peppers
1 tablespoon butter
1 small yellow onion, sliced
1 ripe tomato, cut into quarters
2 tablespoons white rice
2 tablespoons cognac
3 cups Chicken Stock (page 220) or canned chicken broth
½ cup heavy (whipping) cream
Salt, pepper, and cayenne to taste
1 tablespoon chopped fresh parsley
¼ teaspoon paprika

Cut the bell peppers into quarters, discard the cores and seeds, and slice into thin strips. In a large saucepan, melt the butter and sauté the onion until translucent. Add the peppers and tomato and cook over medium-high heat for 5 minutes, stirring frequently. Add the rice and continue cooking for 5 minutes more. Add the cognac and cook for 2 minutes; then add the chicken stock or broth. Bring the soup to a boil, then reduce to a simmer and cook for 20 minutes.

Add the cream to the soup and simmer for an additional 20 minutes. Remove from the heat, transfer to a blender or a food processor, and purée. Strain through a sieve and season with salt, pepper, and cayenne. Ladle into 2 soup bowls and sprinkle with chopped parsley and paprika.

Timberhill Ranch

Steamed Salmon and Asparagus with Orange Sauce

12 medium asparagus spears
One 6-ounce salmon fillet
Salt and pepper to taste
Orange Sauce (recipe follows)
1 orange, peeled and divided into segments for garnish
Mint sprigs for garnish

Trim the asparagus spears to about 5 inches in length. Using a vegetable peeler, slightly peel the stems; then boil the asparagus for 30 seconds in boiling salted water. Remove with a slotted spoon, chill briefly in ice water, and dry with a towel.

Slice the salmon fillet on an extreme bias into ¼-inch thick slices. Gather the asparagus spears into 2 bunches of 6 each and roll a salmon slice around each so that 2 inches of the asparagus tips are still visible. Lightly season with salt and pepper. Place in a steamer basket over boiling water, cover, and steam for 3 minutes, or until just cooked. Remove from the steamer basket carefully.

Serving. Spoon the orange sauce onto 2 plates and place the salmon rolls on top. Garnish with orange segments and mint if you wish and serve immediately.

Orange Sauce

½ cup plus 2 tablespoons fresh orange juice
2 egg whites
2 tablespoons walnut oil
6 tablespoons extra-virgin olive oil
¼ teaspoon pear vinegar
Salt and pepper to taste

Timberhill Ranch

Reserve 2 tablespoons orange juice. In a small saucepan, slowly simmer ½ cup of the orange juice until it reduces to 1 or 2 tablespoons of orange glaze. Remove and chill in the refrigerator.

In a blender or food processor, add the egg white, oils, and vinegar and emulsify at high speed. Add the chilled orange glaze and the remaining 2 tablespoons orange juice, and blend. Season with salt and pepper.

Roasted Breast of Pheasant with Ginger Sesame Glaze

One 3-pound pheasant or roasting chicken
Salt and pepper to taste
Vegetable oil for browning
1 cup Ginger Sesame Glaze (recipe follows)

Preheat the oven to 425° F. Wash and pat the pheasant or chicken dry. Season the bird with salt and pepper, including the cavity. Film the bottom of a sauté pan or skillet with a little vegetable oil over medium-high heat. Add the pheasant or chicken to the pan and quickly brown the bird on each side, then remove and place the pheasant or chicken in a roasting pan. Bake the pheasant or chicken in the preheated oven for 20 minutes. After 20 minutes, remove the pan from the oven and let the bird cool for about 10 minutes.

When the pheasant or chicken is cool enough to handle, bone the breast by cutting alongside the backbone and rib cage, through the wing joint. Remove the breast meat with the wing drumlet intact. Remove the wing tip and second joint and reserve them for stock. Remove the legs and use them for another meal, perhaps a wonderful salad. You may also save the carcass for making stock.

Timberhill Ranch

Place the breast skin side up on a baking sheet and baste with the ginger sesame glace. Return the meat to the oven for 4 minutes and then baste again. After another 4 minutes, sprinkle the breast with sesame seeds and return the meat to the oven for an 5 additional minutes.

Serving. Slice the pheasant breast. Spoon some of the ginger sesame glaze onto 2 plates and lay the slices of pheasant over.

Ginger Sesame Glaze

6 tablespoons honey
2 tablespoons soy sauce
1 tablespoon Asian (toasted) sesame oil
2 tablespoons grated fresh ginger
1 ½ cups Veal Stock (page 226) or reduced canned chicken broth

In a 1-quart saucepan, place the honey, soy sauce, and sesame oil and cook over low heat until the liquid reduces to a glaze, then add the ginger and veal stock or chicken broth. Bring to a boil, then reduce heat and simmer for 20 minutes. Remove from the heat and strain through a sieve.

Spiced Pears with Rum Caramel Sauce

½ cup water

⅓ cup sugar

2 ripe large Bartlett or Bosc pears, peeled, halved lengthwise
(also halve the stems if possible), and cored

1 ½ cups Gewürztraminer wine

One 3-inch cinnamon stick

3 allspice berries

¼ vanilla bean

⅛ teaspoon fresh-grated nutmeg

⅓ cup heavy (whipping) cream

1 tablespoon sifted powdered sugar

¼ teaspoon vanilla extract

Rum Caramel Sauce (recipe follows)

2 mint sprigs, for garnish

In a small saucepan, heat the sugar and water over medium-low heat, stirring to completely dissolve the sugar. When the sugar is just dissolved, remove from heat. Set aside to cool.

Place the pear halves flat side down in a stainless steel or other non-aluminum saucepan. Cover with the sugar syrup, wine, cinnamon stick, and allspice berries. Cut the vanilla bean in half lengthwise. Scrape out the seeds and add the beans and the nutmeg to the pears. The pears should be just covered with liquid; if they're not, add a little water. If necessary, place a heavy object such as a small pot lid on top of the pears to keep them below the surface of the liquid. Simmer over medium heat for 10 minutes, or until just tender when pierced with the tip of a sharp knife. Remove from heat and let cool for 1 hour. Carefully transfer the pears and liquid to a sealed container. Refrigerate until needed.

Just before serving, whip the cream, powdered sugar, and vanilla in a deep bowl until it forms stiff peaks. Place in a pastry bag fitted with a star tip.

Serving. Warm the caramel sauce over low heat. Carefully remove the pears from the liquid with a slotted spoon and place flat side down on a cutting board. With a small sharp knife, make 5 to 7 cuts from stem end to wide end (don't cut through the stem end) so the pears will fan out. Pool some warmed caramel sauce in the center of each of 2 plates. Lift the pears onto the sauce, letting the slices fan out. Garnish with a rosette of whipped cream and a mint sprig.

Note: The pears can be prepared 1 day in advance. The poaching liquid can be saved and used again.

Rum Caramel Sauce

½ cup sugar
¼ cup water
½ cup heavy (whipping) cream
2 tablespoons butter
2 tablespoons dark rum

In a heavy saucepan, combine the sugar and water and bring to a boil over high heat, stirring constantly. Cook at a boil until the caramel turns a golden to medium-brown color. Keep your eye on it because it will turn from light to medium brown very quickly. Carefully remove from the heat (it is extremely hot), and stir in the cream; it will bubble up. When the bubbling stops, return the mixture to the heat, bring to a boil, and stir until smooth. Remove from the heat, add the butter and stir to dissolve; then blend in the rum and cool to room temperature. Refrigerate until needed.

Makes about 1 cup

Note: The rum caramel sauce can be prepared up to a week in advance.

Timberhill Ranch

VENTANA COUNTRY INN RESORT

Big Sur, California

Ventana is a place to relax and recharge the spirit amid some of the world's most spectacular scenery. The Ventana Inn overlooks the dramatic Big Sur coastline of California and is nestled amid 243 acres of grassy meadows and groves of oak and redwood trees. Guests can enjoy strolling along wooded walkways, soaking in soothing Japanese hot baths, saunas, swimming, and a library. Each of the Inn's rooms or suites has its own private balcony or patio. Ventana was recently voted one of the most romantic resorts in the world by *Travel & Leisure* magazine.

The Ventana Restaurant has been awarded the prestigious Mobil Travel Guide Four-Star Award for over ten consecutive years. Gracious dining on California cuisine is enjoyed in the dramatic exposed-beam cedar dining room. The following dinner for two was presented to *Menus and Music* by Ventana chef Peter Charles, and the dessert recipe was created by Ventana pastry chef Elena Steele.

THE MENU

Ventana

Oysters Rockefeller

*Salad of Warm Pear Stuffed with
Stilton Cheese and Walnuts*

*Veal Sauté with Artichokes,
Sun-dried Tomatoes, Pancetta, and Mustard Greens*

Ginger and Lemon Sherbet with Almond Cookies

Ventana Country Inn Resort

Oysters Rockefeller

1 tablespoon clarified butter (page 220)
1 tablespoon minced garlic
1 tablespoon minced shallots
1 tablespoon minced anchovies
2 ½ cups spinach leaves
1 cup stemmed mustard greens, steamed
3 tablespoons pecans, chopped
1 tablespoon Pernod
1 tablespoon grated Romano cheese
Dash cayenne
6 drops Tabasco
8 fresh oysters on the half shell
Rock salt
1 tablespoon heavy (whipping) cream
⅓ cup Hollandaise Sauce (page 223)
4 cups rock salt

Preheat the oven to 450° F. In a sauté pan or skillet, heat the butter and sauté the garlic, shallots, and anchovies for 30 seconds. Add the spinach and mustard greens and sauté until limp. Drain the excess liquid. Transfer to a blender or food processor and add the pecans, Pernod, cheese, cayenne, and Tabasco. Purée until smooth.

Blend together the whipped cream and hollandaise. Shuck the oysters. With a small sharp knife, cut below each oyster to release it from its shell.

Place each oyster in the deeper of its 2 shells and set them on a bed of rock salt in a baking pan. Top each oyster with 1 tablespoon of puréed greens. Bake in the preheated oven for 4 minutes. Top each oyster with 1 teaspoon of creamy hollandaise and bake for 1 minute. Serve immediately.

Ventana Country Inn Resort

Salad of Warm Pear Stuffed with Stilton Cheese and Walnuts

2 cups port wine, or enough to cover the pear halves for poaching
1 pear, peeled, halved, and cored
2 tablespoons Stilton cheese
2 tablespoons walnuts
2 handfuls mixed baby greens
Vinaigrette (recipe follows)
2 tablespoons enoki mushrooms for garnish

Preheat the oven to 400° F. In a medium saucepan, bring the port to a boil. Gently add the pear halves to the port. Reduce the heat to a simmer and poach the pears for 5 to 8 minutes, or until soft when pierced by a sharp knife. Set the pears aside to cool in the port.

In a small bowl, blend together the cheese and walnuts. When the pear halves have cooled, scoop a tablespoon or two from their centers and stuff with the walnut-cheese mixture. In a baking pan, bake the stuffed pears for 4 minutes.

Serving. Toss the greens with the vinaigrette and arrange them on 2 salad plates. Place a stuffed pear half in the center of each plate and garnish with the enoki mushrooms.

Vinaigrette

1 shallot, minced
2 ½ tablespoons pear vinegar
¼ cup walnut oil
Salt and pepper to taste

Whisk together the vinaigrette ingredients.

Ventana Country Inn Resort

Veal Sauté with Artichokes,
Sun-dried Tomatoes, Pancetta, and Mustard Greens

1 ounce pancetta or 1 slice bacon, diced
2 tablespoons clarified butter (page 220)
Four 3-ounce veal medallions, pounded until thin
Flour for dredging
3 tablespoons minced shallots
2 artichoke bottoms, diced (page 159)
4 sun-dried tomatoes, blanched and dried
⅔ cup packed stemmed and diced mustard greens
¼ cup sherry wine vinegar
½ cup Veal Stock (page 226) or reduced canned chicken broth
4 tablespoons unsalted butter
Salt and pepper to taste

In a heavy sauté pan or skillet, sauté the pancetta or bacon over medium-low heat until just crisp, about 10 minutes. Drain on paper towels and set aside.

In a sauté pan or skillet, melt the butter over high heat. Dip the veal medallions in flour until lightly covered, sauté for 1 minute, then turn and sauté 1 more minute on the other side.

Drain off most of the butter and add the shallots, artichoke bottoms, sun-dried tomatoes, pancetta or bacon, mustard greens, vinegar, and veal stock or chicken broth. Stir and cook until the mustard greens and shallots are limp. Remove the veal and set aside. Continue cooking the sauce over high heat for 30 seconds to reduce, then stir in the butter, salt, and pepper.

Serving. Spoon the sauce onto 2 dinner plates and arrange the veal medallions on top. Serve immediately with your choice of vegetables and rice.

Ventana Country Inn Resort

Ginger and Lemon Sherbet with
Almond Cookies

¾ cup plus 2 tablespoons sugar
½ cup plus 2 tablespoons water
1 teaspoon grated lemon zest (page 86)
⅔ cup sparkling mineral water
1 tablespoon fresh lemon juice
1 ½ teaspoons minced candied ginger
Almond Cookies (recipe follows)

In a medium saucepan, combine the sugar, water, and lemon zest and bring to a boil. Remove from the heat and let cool. When the mixture has cooled, stir in the mineral water and lemon juice. Freeze in an ice cream maker following the manufacturer's intructions. When almost set, add the ginger and continue freezing until set.

Almond Cookies

½ cup sliced unblanched almonds
½ cup sugar
2 tablespoons unbleached all-purpose flour
1 egg white

In a mixing bowl, combine all the ingredients until thoroughly blended. Refrigerate the dough for 1 hour.

Preheat the oven to 300° F. Butter and flour a baking sheet, and drop the dough by large tablespoonfuls on the sheet. Bake for 8 minutes, or until golden.

Ventana Country Inn Resort

THE WHITE BARN INN

Kennebunkport, Maine

In the 1800s, travelers exploring Maine's rugged coastline often made their way to the old Boothby boardinghouse in Kennebunkport, Maine. They found a warm welcome, comfortable lodging, and an "excellent table." From these simple beginnings, the homestead has evolved into the White Barn Inn, which offers luxurious accommodations, a renowned restaurant, and the same warm welcome that greeted travelers of long ago. Besides membership in Relais & Chateaux, the inn has been awarded the Four-Diamond Award from the American Automobile Association.

The White Barn Inn has twenty-five meticulously restored guest rooms decorated with period furnishings from the mid-eighteenth century. Guests can bicycle along a stunning stretch of coastline, enjoy ocean swims, wander a nearby beach, explore miles of woodland trails, or take a five-minute stroll to the town of Kennebunkport, with its mulititude of fine shops, galleries, and antiques stores.

The White Barn Inn's restaurant enjoys a widespread reputation for excellent New England cooking. The sumptuous offerings change with the season, with a special focus always on the seafood caught by local fishermen. Two restored barns on the property make a convivial setting for meals, or if a more traditional and intimate atmosphere is preferred, the dining room in the main house offers a pleasing alternative. The following dinner for two from the White Barn Inn was presented to *Menus and Music* by chef Richard Lemoine.

The White Barn Inn

THE MENU

White Barn Inn

Fruits from the Maine Coastline

Scallops with Bacon and Maple Dijon Cream

Oysters on the Half Shell with
Cranberries, Orange Zest, and Cracked White Peppercorns

Grilled Maine Lobster
with Tarragon Succotash

Ginger Crêpes with Cinnamon Pastry Cream
and Chunky Applesauce

The White Barn Inn

Scallops with Bacon and Maple Dijon Cream

One ¼-inch bacon slab, or 2 bacon slices
8 sea scallops*
1 tablespoon peanut oil
Minced fresh snipped chive blossoms or fresh chives for garnish
Maple Dijon Cream (recipe follows)

Cut the bacon slab or bacon slices into ⅛-inch strips and sauté in a sauté pan or skillet until crisp. Dry on paper towels and set aside.

Wash the scallops and pat them dry with paper towels. Heat a heavy sauté pan or skillet until very hot and add the peanut oil. Lightly season the scallops with salt and pepper and sauté for about 1 minute on each side, leaving them slightly underdone.

Serving. Ladle about 4 tablespoons of warm maple Dijon cream onto each of 2 serving plates. (A scallop dish makes a nice presentation.) Divide the scallops between the plates. Garnish with the cooked bacon pieces and chive blossoms or chives. Serve at once.

*The White Barn Inn uses Maine "diver's scallops," and these are the preferred ingredient. These scallops are caught along the northern Maine coast, and are hand picked by divers, as opposed to being dragged.

The White Barn Inn

Maple Dijon Cream

1 teaspoon butter
1 shallot, minced
2 tablespoons brandy
1 cup heavy (whipping) cream
1 tablespoon Dijon mustard
¼ cup maple syrup
Coarse sea salt and white pepper to taste

In a small, heavy saucepan, melt the butter and sauté the shallot until soft. Add the brandy and stir over high heat for 1 minute. Add the cream and boil to reduce to about ¾ cup. Stir in the mustard and maple syrup. Bring to a boil and reduce again until thick enough to coat the back of a spoon.

Oysters on the Half Shell with Cranberries, Orange Zest, and Cracked White Peppercorns

3 cups water
¼ cup sugar
1 orange
½ cup fresh whole cranberries, rinsed
1 tablespoon white peppercorns, cracked
2 tablespoons cider vinegar
6 oysters,* washed

In a small saucepan, bring 2 cups of the water and the sugar to a boil, stirring to dissolve the sugar. Remove from the heat and set aside to let cool.

With a sharp knife or a zester, cut the orange zest from the orange, leaving the white pith. Cut the orange zest into thin julienne strips.

In a small saucepan, bring the remaining 1 cup of water to a boil and add the orange zest. When the water returns to a boil, remove the zest with a slotted spoon and transfer to a bowl of ice water to stop the cooking. Repeat this process twice.

In a small saucepan, place 1 cup of the sugar syrup and the orange zest. Bring to a boil, remove the pan from the heat, and set aside to let cool.

In a small saucepan, bring the remaining sugar syrup to a boil. Add the cranberries and cook until you hear the berries begin to pop. Remove from the heat, and set aside to cool.

In a small bowl, combine the cracked peppercorns and cider vinegar. Open the oysters, severing the muscle from the shell. Discard the shallow half shells, retaining the deeper shells to serve the oysters.

Serving. Present the oysters on the half shell on crushed ice. Spoon some of the vinegar and peppercorns onto each oyster. Top with several drained cranberries and sprinkle with a few drained orange zest threads. Serve very cold.

Note: The orange zest and cranberries can be covered and refrigerated for weeks. Use to garnish puddings, sherbets, and fruit desserts.

*The White Barn Inn uses Permaquid oysters, and these are preferred ingredient if you can find them.

The White Barn Inn

Grilled Maine Lobster with Tarragon Succotash

Two 1 ½-pound live lobsters
Tarragon Succotash (recipe follows)
Tarragon sprigs for garnish

Light a charcoal fire in an open grill. In a large stockpot, boil enough salted water to cover the 2 lobsters. Add the lobsters to the boiling water, cover, and cook for 8 minutes; remove and place in ice water to stop the cooking process. Reserve the pot of cooking water. Remove all the meat from the lobster, which will be under-cooked. Make 3 slashes across the underside of the tails to straighten them.

On a flat work surface, lay out 2 corn husks, then lay another husk on top of each to make 2 layers. Divide the lobster meat between the doubled husks, placing the meat at the bottom end of each doubled husk. Fold in the sides of each doubled husk and roll the husks to completely seal the meat; tie each roll with a piece of cotton string. Set aside 1 cup of the reserved lobster cooking water for the succotash. Place the rolled husks in the remaining water to soak for 30 minutes before cooking.

Grill the lobster husks for 1½ minutes on each side, then cook for an additional 5 minutes on each side. Remove from the grill.

Serving. Remove the string and the charred outer husk from the lobster, leaving the inner husk to retain the steam. Place in the center of a warm plate. Spoon the succotash around the lobster. Garnish with tarragon sprigs and serve immediately.

*Dried corn husks may be found in Latino markets and some large supermarkets.

Tarragon Succotash

1 ear fresh corn
1 cup lima beans
½ pound fresh green beans
1 cup reserved lobster broth from previous recipe
2 tablespoons butter
Salt and cayenne pepper to taste
1 tablespoon chopped fresh tarragon

Shuck the corn moments before cooking it. Pull the husk off the ear and remove the silk. Cook the corn in boiling salted water to cover for 3 to 5 minutes, or until tender. Cut the kernels from the cob with a sharp knife; you should have 1 cup. Blanch the green beans and lima beans in boiling salted water to cover for about 1 minute; remove with a slotted spoon and chill in cold water to stop the cooking process. Chop the green beans into bite-sized pieces. In a mixing bowl, combine the corn, lima beans, and green beans; set aside.

In a medium saucepan, heat the reserved lobster broth, add the vegetables, and cook until heated through. Add the butter and season with salt and cayenne pepper. Add the chopped tarragon and serve immediately.

The White Barn Inn

Ginger Crêpes with Cinnamon Pastry Cream and Chunky Applesauce

Ginger Crêpes

1 cup water
2 cups sugar
2 tablespoons sliced fresh ginger
½ cup unbleached all-purpose flour
1 egg
½ cup milk
2 teaspoons butter, melted
1 teaspoon brown sugar

In a small, heavy saucepan, bring the water and sugar to a boil, and cook, stirring occasionally, for 3 minutes. Add the ginger and cook until it is soft when pierced by a sharp knife. Remove the ginger with a slotted spoon, cool, and cut into small julienne.

In a blender or food processor, place the flour, egg, milk, melted butter, and brown sugar. Process until smooth, then stir in the ginger. Transfer to a container and refrigerate the batter for 1 hour.

Cinnamon Pastry Cream

1 ½ cups milk
1 vanilla bean, split
1 cinnamon stick, cracked
5 egg yolks
⅓ cup sugar
2 tablespoons butter

The White Barn Inn

In a small saucepan over medium-low heat, place the milk, seeds from the vanilla bean, and cinnamon stick and bring to a simmer. Remove the pan from the heat, cover, and set aside for 15 minutes. Strain through a sieve. Return the milk to a pan and reheat.

In medium saucepan, whisk together the egg yolks and sugar until foamy. Slowly add the warm milk to the eggs while whisking constantly. Return to heat and whisk until the mixture thickens enough to coat the back of a spoon. Remove from heat, add the butter, and let cool.

Note: This pastry cream may be made ahead and refrigerated for several days.

Chunky Applesauce

4 apples, peeled, cored, and diced
1 tablespoon fresh lemon juice
2 tablespoons maple syrup
1 teaspoon ground cinnamon
¼ teaspoon ground cloves

In a medium saucepan, combine all the ingredients over medium heat and cook until the apples soften. Remove from the heat and cool. In a blender or food processor, add the apple mixture and purée. Set aside.

Note: When the applesauce is cool, it may be covered and refrigerated for several days.

Cooking and Serving

clarified butter (page 220) for cooking crêpes
¼ cup grated Maine or other Cheddar cheese

The White Barn Inn

Heat a nonstick sauté pan or skillet over medium-high heat. Brush the bottom of the pan with clarified butter and pour off any extra butter. Ladle 2 tablespoons of the crêpe batter into the pan, and rotate the pan to spread the batter into a thin pancake. When the crêpe is dry on top, flip it over and allow it to finish cooking on the other side. Remove from the pan and cool. Repeat until all the batter is used. Allow each crêpe to cool before stacking.

Serving. Spoon pastry cream into the center of each crêpe and roll. Place the filled crêpes on 2 dessert plates and spoon warm chunky applesauce over. Sprinkle with grated Cheddar cheese.

BASICS

Chicken Stock

8 cups or so raw and/or cooked chicken bones and scraps
Water to cover by 1 inch
2 teaspoons salt
1 onion, chopped
3 celery stalks, chopped
8 parsley sprigs
Salt and freshly ground pepper to taste

Chop the bones and scraps into small pieces and bring to the simmer in a 3-quart saucepan with the water and salt. Skim off any foam that rises to the surface. Add the onion, celery, carrots, and parsley. Cover the pan and simmer for 1 hour, adding water to keep the ingredients covered. Strain through a sieve into a bowl and refrigerate. Scrape off any surface fat that congeals on top. Season with salt and pepper before using.

Makes about 2 quarts

Note: This stock will keep several days in a covered container in the refrigerator. To freeze, pour into a plastic container and seal well; chicken stock will keep for 2 months in the refrigerator.

Clarified Butter

½ cup (1 stick) butter

Cut the butter into small pieces for quick melting. In a heavy saucepan, melt the butter over low heat until it crackles and bubbles. Remove the pan from the heat and use a spoon to carefully skim off the foamy butterfat that has risen to the surface. Pour the clear yellow liquid into a container, leaving the milky residue at the bottom; cover. The butter will keep for months in the refrigerator or freezer.

Crème Fraîche

1 cup heavy (whipping) cream
2 tablespoons buttermilk or yogurt

Combine the cream and buttermilk or yogurt in a glass container and let sit at room temperature (70° to 80° F) 5 to 8 hours or overnight to thicken. Refrigerate in a covered container.

Makes 1 cup

Note: The advantage of crème fraîche over sour cream is that it can be boiled and reduced without curdling. It will keep in the refrigerator for about 1 week.

Duck Stock

3 pounds duck bones and trimmings
1 cup dry red wine
1 onion, chopped
1 large carrot, peeled and chopped
1 celery stalk, chopped
1 leek, chopped
9 parsley sprigs

Preheat the oven to 450° F. In a roasting pan, brown the bones and trimmings, turning once or twice, for 30 minutes or until the bones and trimmings are a deep brown. Transfer to a large saucepan or kettle and drain the fat from the roasting pan.

Deglaze the roasting pan with the wine and add the pan juices to the bones. Add the onion, carrot, celery, leek, and parsley to the bones. Add water to cover by 1 inch and bring to a boil over high heat. Skim the surface to remove any foam that rises to the top. Reduce to a simmer and cook uncovered for 3 to 4 hours. Add water as needed to keep the ingredients covered.

Strain through a sieve and refrigerate. Remove any congealed fat that rises to the surface.

Makes about 6 cups (1quart)

Note: This stock will keep 2 or 3 days in a covered container in the refrigerator. To freeze, pour into a plastic container and seal well; duck stock will keep for 2 months in the freezer.

Fish Stock

1 quart fish heads, bones, and trimmings
1 stalk celery, chopped
1 onion, chopped
1 carrot, peeled and chopped
1 bay leaf
4 parsley sprigs
Salt and pepper to taste

Wash the fish parts well. In a large pot, place the fish, celery, onion, carrot, bay leaf, parsley, and water to cover by 1 inch. Bring to a boil and skim off the foam as it rises to the surface. Cover and simmer for 20 minutes.

Remove from the heat and strain through a sieve. Adjust the seasoning with salt and pepper.

Basics

Makes about 4 cups

Note: To refrigerate or freeze, pour the cooled stock into a plastic container and seal well. Fish stock will keep a day or two in the refrigerator and 2 months in the freezer.

Hollandaise Sauce

3 egg yolks
2 tablespoons fresh lemon juice
½ cup (1 stick) unsalted butter, melted
Salt and ground white pepper to taste

Place the egg yolks in a blender or food processor and add the lemon juice. Blend the egg yolks and, with the motor running, pour in half of the melted butter in a very thin stream; the yolks will emulsify to a thick sauce. Remove the sauce from the blender or food processor and slowly whisk in the remaining melted butter. Season with salt and pepper.

Makes about 1 cup

Lamb Stock

Uncooked bones and trimmings from a boned leg of lamb
1 carrot, peeled and chopped
1 onion, chopped
1 cup water
Salt and pepper to taste
1 celery stalk, chopped
2 garlic cloves, smashed
1 bay leaf
¼ teaspoon chopped fresh rosemary

Preheat the oven to 425° F. In a roasting pan, brown the bones and trimmings with the carrot and onion for 30 to 40 minutes, turning occasionally. Transfer the bones and vegetables to a saucepan or kettle and drain the fat from the roasting pan.

Deglaze the roasting pan with the water, and pour this liquid into the pot with the bones. Add water to cover the ingredients by 1 inch and bring to the simmer. Skim off any foam that rises to the surface. Season with salt and pepper. Add the chopped celery, garlic, bay leaf, and rosemary. Cover and simmer for 3 to 4 hours. Add water as needed to keep the ingredients covered.

Strain through a sieve into a bowl and refrigerate. Spoon off the congealed fat that rises to the top.

Makes about 2 quarts

Note: To refrigerate or freeze, pour the cooled stock into a plastic container and seal well. This stock will keep several days in the refrigerator and 2 months in the freezer.

Basics

Pie Pastry

½ cup (1 stick) butter
1 ½ cups unbleached all-purpose flour
¼ teaspoon salt
3 to 4 tablespoons cold water

With a pastry cutter or 2 knives, cut the butter into the flour and salt until crumbly, or process for 10 seconds in a food processor. Sprinkle in the water and mix with a fork, then press together in a ball (or process for 20 seconds in a food processor). Allow the dough to rest in the refrigerator for at least 30 minutes before rolling out.

Makes one 9-inch pie shell

Toasted Hazelnuts

½ cup hazelnuts

Preheat the oven to 350° F. Spread the nuts on a jelly-roll pan or baking sheet and bake for 10 to 15 minutes, tossing them several times. They are done when lightly browned. Remove from the oven and rub in a rough towel or double thickness of paper towels to remove the skins.

Note: Toasting hazelnuts gives them much added flavor. When thoroughly cool, place nuts into a covered container and freeze.

Veal Stock

2 pounds veal bones
2 tablespoons oil
1 onion, chopped
1 carrot, peeled and chopped
1 celery stalk, chopped
½ cup dry white wine
Salt and pepper to taste

Preheat the oven to 400° F. In a roasting pan, toss the bones with the oil and vegetables. Brown for 30 to 40 minutes, turning occasionally. Transfer the bones and vegetables to a large saucepan or kettle.

Pour the fat out of the roasting pan, and deglaze the pan with the wine. Pour this liquid into the saucepan with the bones and vegetables. Add water to cover the ingredients by 1 inch. Bring to a boil and skim off any foam that rises to the top. Add salt and pepper, cover, and simmer 3 to 4 hours.

Strain through a sieve into a bowl and refrigerate. Remove any congealed fat that rises to the surface.

Makes about 1 quart

Note: This stock will keep several days in a covered container in the refrigerator. To freeze, pour into a plastic container and seal well; veal stock will keep for 2 months in the freezer.

Basics

Vegetable Broth

2 carrots, peeled and chopped
2 celery stalks, chopped
1 green bell pepper, cored, seeded, and chopped
2 medium zucchini, chopped
1 small onion, chopped
1 ½ cups chopped green beans
2 cups chopped leeks
1 cup peeled and chopped parsnips
12 ounces fresh spinach, stemmed
4 dill sprigs
1 bay leaf
2 garlic cloves, peeled
1 teaspoon salt
1 teaspoon freshly ground black pepper
3 quarts water

Combine all the ingredients in a large kettle and bring to a boil. Reduce the heat and simmer, uncovered, for 30 minutes. Remove from the heat and let sit for 30 minutes. Strain through a sieve, pressing out as much liquid from the vegetables as possible; discard the vegetables. Return to the heat and simmer for 30 minutes.

Makes about 6 cups

Note: This broth will keep several days in a covered container in the refrigerator. To freeze, pour into a plastic container and seal well.

CONVERSION CHARTS

Weight Measurements

Standard U.S.	Ounces	Metric
1 ounce	1	28 g
¼ lb	4	113 g
½ lb	8	226 g
1 lb	16	454 g
1½ lb	24	680 g
2 lb	37	908 g
2½ lb	40	1134 g
3 lb	48	1367 g

Volume Measurements

Standard U.S.		Ounces	Metric
1 tbs		½	15 ml
2 tbs		1	30 ml
3 tbs		½	45 ml
¼ cup	4 tbs	2	60 ml
6 tbs		3	85 ml
½ cup	8 tbs	4	115 ml
1 cup		8	240 ml
2 cups	1 pint	16	480 ml
4 cups	1 quart	32	960 ml

Conversion Charts

Oven Temperatures

Fahrenheit	Celsius
300°	148.8°
325°	162.8°
350°	177°
375°	190.5°
400°	204.4°
425°	218.3°
450°	232°

Conversion Factors

Ounces to grams: Multiply the ounce figure by 28.3 to get the number of grams.

Pounds to grams: Multiply the pound figure by 453.59 to get the number of grams.

Pounds to kilograms: Multiply the pound figure by 0.45 to get the number of kilograms.

Ounces to milliliters: Multiply the ounce figure by 30 to get the number of milliliters.

Cups to liters: Multiply the cup figure by 0.24 to get the number of liters.

Fahrenheit to Celsius: Subtract 32 from the Fahrenheit figure, multiply by 5, then divide by 9 to get the Celsius figure.

ALPHABETICAL LIST OF INNS AND RESORTS

Bermuda

Horizons and Cottages
P.O. Box PG 198
Paget West, PG BX
Bermuda
(809) 236-0048

Canada

Hastings House
P.O. Box 1110
Ganges, British Columbia
Canada V0S 1E0
(604) 537-2362

The Inn at Manitou
McKellar Center Road
McKellar, Ontario
Canada P0G 1C0
(705) 389-2171

Langdon Hall
Rural Route 33
Cambridge, Ontario
Canada N3H 4R8
(519) 740-2100

The Millcroft Inn
P.O. Box 89
John Street
Alton, Ontario
Canada L0N 1A0
(416) 791-4422

United States

Auberge du Soleil
180 Rutherford Hill Road
Rutherford, California 94573
(707) 963-1211

Blantyre
Rural Route 20
Lenox, Massachusetts 01240
(413) 637-3556

The Fearrington House
2000 Fearrington Village
  Center
Pittsboro, North Carolina
  27312
(919) 542-2121

Hotel Hana-Maui
P.O. Box 8
Hana, Maui
Hawaii 96713
(808) 248-8211

The Home Ranch
P.O. Box 822-R
Clark, Colorado 80428
(303) 879-1780

The Inn at Little Washington
P.O. Box 300
Middle and Main Streets
Washington, Virginia 22747
(703) 675-3800

The Inn at Sawmill Farm
P.O. Box 367
Rural Route 100
Mt. Snow Valley
West Dover, Vermont 05356
(802) 464-8131

La Colombe d'Or
3410 Montrose Boulevard
Houston, Texas 77006
(713) 524-7999

Meadowood Resort Hotel
900 Meadowood Lane
St. Helena, California
  94574
(707) 963-3646

The Point
Star Route
Saranac Lake, New York
  12983
(518) 891-5678

San Ysidro Ranch
900 San Ysidro Lane
Montecito, California
  93108
(805) 969-5046

The Sherman House
2160 Green Street
San Francisco, California
  94123
(415) 563-3600

Timberhill Ranch
35755 Hauser Bridge Road
Cazadero, California 95421
(707) 847-3258

Ventana Big Sur
Big Sur, California 93920
(408) 667-2331

The White Barn Inn
P.O. Box 560-C
Beach Street
Kennebunkport, Maine
  04046
(207) 967-2321

INDEX

Index

Index

Index

Index

Index

Sharon O'Connor is a musician, author, and cook. The cellist and founder of the San Francisco String Quartet, she has performed with the quartet for more than twelve years and enjoys experiencing firsthand the combination of beautiful music and fine food. The *Menus and Music* series combines her love of music, food, and travel. *Dinners for Two* is her fifth book.